Praise for *The Id*

"The general format of the book is user friendly with a logical flow of chapters covering the entire process from idea to starting your own business. There a number of potential users of this guide: would-be entrepreneurs, inventors, business advisors and educators of entrepreneurship. All could benefit from having *"The Idea Guide"* as part of their reference library. The workbook format is easy to work through and ensures a strong start to any budding enterprise."

THE INNOVATION CENTRE

"...the step by step format is thorough and easy to follow. Any business person who wants to start a new business or implement a new idea or product line in an existing business would benefit from reading this book The Idea Guide provides a planning and development process which is practical and which should increase the chances for business success."

ASSOCIATION OF WOMEN
ENTREPRENEURS AND EXECUTIVES

"...the examples given add more reality to the book. These are not included in other business development books Anyone considering starting a business could benefit from the practical layout of the book, its self evaluation component and the planning questions. It gives entrepreneurs an opportunity to better understand what they need to consider in starting a new business."

GLOBAL ENTREPRENEURSHIP CENTRE

"A refreshing characteristic of *The Idea Guide* is its practical format...overall the concise book provides an inexpensive, risk-free assessment and preparation of a business, potentially saving much time effort and money associated with startup or expensive outside consultation."

BUSINESS NETWORK MAGAZINE

"It is an excellent straight forward resource for someone to plan and start their own business. It has a balance of being thorough without being overwhelming."

WOMEN AND RURAL ECONOMIC DEVELOPMENT

"David Ceolin has made the planning process less daunting by presenting it in the form of a step-by-step tutorial that is straight forward, user friendly, and accessible to readers of all levels of business knowledge and expertise. If you are in need of a comprehensive business planning guide that will ask you all the right questions to help you assess and develop your business, *The Idea Guide* is an excellent resource."

YOUNG ENTREPRENEURS ASSOCIATION

"...the book allows the reader to quickly evaluate any type of business idea and develop an effective plan before risking the start-up costs..."

The Times

"With proper planning anything is possible. *The Idea Guide* is the catalyst for taking ideas and dreams, and putting them to action."

ASSOCIATION OF COLLEGIATE ENTREPRENEURS

The Idea Guide

**The step-by-step guide for planning
and running your own business**

by David Ceolin

Otabind (Ota-bind). this book has been bound
using the patented Otabind process. You can open
this book at any page, gently run your fingers down
the spine, and the pages will lie flat. Otabind combines
improved book binding adhesive technology
with a unique free floating cover to produce a
reader friendly book.
In addition to being more enjoyable to read or work
with than other books that won't stay open, Otabind
books are uncommonly durable.

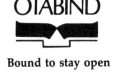

Bound to stay open

The Idea Guide

The step-by-step guide for planning and running your own business

by David Ceolin

Canadian Cataloguing in Publication Data

Ceolin, David, date

The idea guide : the step-by-step guide for planning and running your own business

Includes index.

ISBN 0-9699498-0-4

1. New business enterprises-Planning.

2. Small business-Planning. 3. Entrepreneurship.

I. Envision Communications Ltd.   II. Title.

HD62.5.C46 1995   658.1'1 C95-931099-l

Published by Envision Communications Ltd., Toronto
(for additional helpful and practical small business information visit *The Idea Guide* website *at www.ideaguide.com*)

Printed and bound in Canada
Fourth Edition
Editor: Tom McGee
Page and Cover Design: Steven Schorsch, Retina Productions, and Bryan Leblanc-Whiterock Communications

About the Author

David Ceolin heads Envision Communications Ltd., a firm headquartered in Toronto that provides entrepreneurial training and information to corporations, educational institutions, and governments.

His practical experience with small business and entrepreneurs began several years ago as a business loans manager with a major chartered bank. In this capacity he worked with a diversity of business startups and existing companies encompassing a wide variety of pursuits in retail, service, manufacturing, importing, exporting, and technology.

As a banker, Mr. Ceolin evaluated the performance of businesses on a daily basis to help analyze their potential for success and financing. As a business owner, he knows firsthand the crucial steps of preparation required of an individual wishing to start and operate a business successfully.

The experience resulting from his varied roles in small business gives him a unique appreciation of the needs of a prospective entrepreneur. Consequently, *The Idea Guide* is practical and concise. The information that must be considered to properly evaluate and plan a business idea is summarized in an easy-to-read format that avoids unnecessary technical business and legal jargon. The essential steps for preparing and starting a business are explained in these pages.

The steps covered in the pages of *The Idea Guide* are essential for prospective business owners who understand that preparation is the key ingredient to a successful, rewarding business experience.

Acknowledgements

I would like to thank the many entrepreneurs who have offered their insights and opinions over the years on what it takes to start and operate a successful business.

Several individuals provided constructive feedback on the concept or the original drafts and each in their own way made the book a better read. These people included (in alphabetical order) Scott Campbell, Eaton Donald, Leslie English, Jennifer Fargey, Jim Fargey, Mel Gardner, Paul Godman, Martin Lucyk, Lorraine Kelly, Michael Kelly, Bill Matz, Tom Martin, Steven Schorsch, Peter Shirriff, Lloyd Taylor, and Stuart Weinstein.

A special thanks to Tom McGee, my editor, for his patience in tackling this project and having the insight to suggest key adjustments that allow the finished product to communicate effectively.

As anyone who is considering going forward with an idea knows, it helps to have individuals to cheer you on. My family members have always provided a reassuring belief in my endeavours. My friends have given me their patience, moral support, and inspiration, all of which help complete any project. Finally, a very special thank you to my wife whose love and encouragement made this idea possible.

FOREWORD

Moving a Business Idea Forward

"A mind once stretched by a new idea, never regains its original dimensions".
Oliver Wendell Holmes

Each one of us has had a good business idea at one time or another. They can be ideas to start a business, make improvements to an existing business, or help others such as employers or community groups plan their operations better. Business ideas can relate to retail, service, franchise, or manufacturing opportunities. They can even be run from home on a full-time or part-time basis.

While we have all had ideas, they often come and go quickly or sit in the back of our minds waiting to be thought out. Many of us have probably had the experience of seeing someone else start the business idea that we had brilliantly thought of years previously (but didn't do anything about). The idea for this book came about to address this idea development and preparation process. Its goal is to provide readers with a concise proven format to thoroughly organize, evaluate, plan, and run a business and keep it healthy long after startup.

When we think of a business idea, it is often related to a hobby or skill that we possess or an opportunity that we have discovered that others could use. It is exciting to wonder what it would be like to start and independently run such a business. Actually developing and planning the idea on paper and seeing your idea take shape can similarly be an enjoyable, inspiring process.

However, some people ignore this simple preparation stage and dive into starting a business, turning what should be one of the most enjoyable experiences of their lives into a sea of wasted money, time, and effort. These people make up the vast majority of the business failure statistics that we all hear about.

Builders follow a blueprint in construction to eliminate the possibility of errors, wasted time, wasted effort and wasted money. The resulting structure that is erected is safe thereby minimizing risk of potential problems. Similarly, preparing beforehand can become your blueprint to develop the business idea more thoroughly and reduce wasted time, effort and money.

Using *The Idea Guide* will prepare you for the important business issues that make a business successful such as setting the right price, identifying how trends affect your idea, planning effective promotion, meeting any competition, and determining the best form of ownership to suit your situation. If you require financing to help you start the business, a bank or other lender will insist on a well-thought out plan (if you are wondering why, turn to Appendix B to see how banks make their loan decisions and how you can prepare). *The Idea Guide* helps you prepare a plan that is preferred by investors and banks.

The Idea Guide provides you with everything you need to prepare and start the idea. Most importantly, it will serve as your own custom reference manual containing the key business issues that must be considered before and after starting a business.

D.C.

TABLE OF CONTENTS

About the Author
Acknowledgments
Foreword
Introduction: How to Use *The Idea Guide*

Chapters

APPENDICES

INDEX

INTRODUCTION

How to Use The Idea Guide

The Idea Guide guides you step-by-step through the business issues that should be addressed to properly evaluate your business idea, develop it further, start it up as a business and run it successfully. Each step of the workbook is set up like a mini-tutorial which covers a separate business issue. There are <u>four parts to each step</u> as shown in the example below.

1) *T*he first part of each step introduces a key business issue in planning the business idea and running a business.

2) *A* business example demonstrating the business issue covered in the step.

3) *Q*uestions relate each business issue to your idea and can be answered in the workbook. Answers become the content for your own custom plan (and questions not answered can help signify areas of the idea requiring futher development)

4) *T*he insights and requirements of an outside "Evaluator", who could be a potential partner, lender, customer, etc., and tips on addressing their requirements.

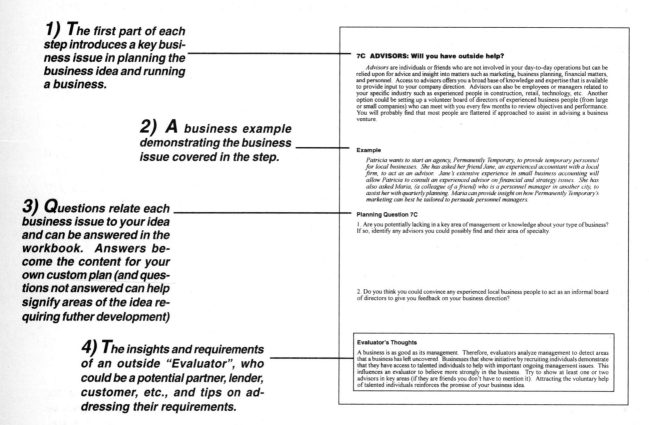

7C ADVISORS: Will you have outside help?

Advisors are individuals or friends who are not involved in your day-to-day operations but can be relied upon for advice and insight into matters such as marketing, business planning, financial matters, and personnel. Access to advisors offers you a broad base of knowledge and expertise that is available to provide input to your company direction. Advisors can also be employees or managers related to your specific industry such as experienced people in construction, retail, technology, etc. Another option could be setting up a volunteer board of directors of experienced business people (from large or small companies) who can meet with you every few months to review objectives and performance. You will probably find that most people are flattered if approached to assist in advising a business venture.

Example

Patricia wants to start an agency, Permanently Temporary, to provide temporary personnel for local businesses. She has asked her friend Jane, an experienced accountant with a local firm, to act as an advisor. Jane's extensive experience in small business accounting will allow Patricia to consult an experienced advisor on financial and strategy issues. She has also asked Maria, (a colleague of a friend) who is a personnel manager in another city, to assist her with quarterly planning. Maria can provide insight on how Permanently Temporary's marketing can best be tailored to persuade personnel managers.

Planning Question 7C

1. Are you potentially lacking in a key area of management or knowledge about your type of business? If so, identify any advisors you could possibly find and their area of specialty.

2. Do you think you could convince any experienced local business people to act as an informal board of directors to give you feedback on your business direction?

Evaluator's Thoughts

A business is as good as its management. Therefore, evaluators analyze management to detect areas that a business has left uncovered. Businesses that show initiative by recruiting individuals demonstrate that they have access to talented individuals to help with important ongoing management issues. This influences an evaluator to believe more strongly in the business. Try to show at least one or two advisors in key areas (if they are friends you don't have to mention it). Attracting the voluntary help of talented individuals reinforces the promise of your business idea.

Each step provokes your thoughts on how the particular issue might be related to your idea. These thoughts and other information that you gather along the way can be recorded within each step of the workbook format allowing you to organize your information in one place (the steps are arranged in the exact order of a standard business plan so that you will actually complete a draft plan by working through the steps). The resulting information will allow you to evaluate your idea and provide you with a thorough plan to achieve your objectives for starting a business.

The easiest way to use the guide is to *read the step, refer to the example,* and *record any thoughts* of how the issue may relate to your idea by answering the questions. Others may prefer to set up a binder with ten sections (one for each chapter) to record their answers. Either way is effective.

While the guide is very instructional in guiding you through the necessary steps to develop a plan, keep in mind that any thoughts or answers that you initially have are valuable and can be refined as you go. This is made easier by comparing your answers to the *"Evaluator's Thoughts."* Think of an evaluator of your plan as a banker, consultant, potential partner, manager, supplier, investor, customer, friend, or parent. All of these individuals would want to understand your business idea better before supporting or becoming involved with it. Comparing your answers to *evaluators'* perspectives will make your idea stronger. Should you intend to actually approach an evaluator, the guide provides you with everything you need to show them.

HOW TO PROCEED THROUGH THE GUIDE

Keep in mind that developing your idea is a process, one that does not necessarily require the conventional structure that people try to attach to many other activities. After going through the guide you may even find that what your idea looks like at the end is completely different than what you initially envisioned. This is normal evolution of a business idea.

Although there is no structured way or time length within which to complete this guide, it does build on some simple principles in the beginning. If you are early in your thought process, try starting at Chapter 1 and proceeding step by step chapter by chapter. You can jump around from section to section as one section may spark you to think of information applicable for another area. Chapters 1, 2, and 3 allow you to discuss the basic foundation of your idea and the potential market for it. These three chapters alone will help you see your idea in a different way. The rest of the book helps you fill in the details to support the idea.

HOW TO GATHER INFORMATION

Much of the information will come from your own thoughts as you read the sections. However, if you cannot initially answer a question, don't worry about it. Filling in details of a business idea can be the result of various pieces of information. A conversation, a read of a newspaper, or even a shopping trip may all provide you with further material and ideas to round out your own idea. Example: You are out comparing cars before purchasing and you decide that a warranty is an important criteria in the purchase decision. Perhaps you could similarly offer a warranty or guarantee with your business idea so that your potential customers can similarly be influenced to choose you over others? Observing all other types of business (which should be easy since we interact everyday with some type of business) will produce a vast amount of valuable information to improve and develop your own idea and keep your business constantly improving after startup.

If you cannot answer a question, skip it until you find the information you need to complete it. Skipped questions can help indicate an area that needs to be considered before going forward, making your idea stronger when you do begin. The first appendix in the back of the book (Appendix A **How To Gather Information**) may help steer you in the direction where you can find any missing details. Answering the questions throughout the guide in point form is easiest. You can make these answers into your own plan by following the steps below.

WHAT TO DO AFTER COMPLETING THE STEPS

Once you have put as much information as you can into each step, you should put it all together in one written document (to create your own custom blueprint or *business plan*) to guide yourself. This business plan can also be presented to others who may have an interest in what you are doing (having it in one document allows them to also provide you with valuable feedback). There may be various individuals who require you to submit your business plan to them. As mentioned, these could be potential partners or financiers such as relatives, friends, family, banks, or investors.

The appendix at the end of the book (**Appendix B: The Uses of Your Plan**) guides you through the simple process of turning your answers into a business plan and offers tips on making your finished plan communicate effectively. Following the instructions will allow you to create an effective plan for your needs and in a format accepted by investors and lenders, including banks.

VISIT THE IDEA GUIDE WEBSITE (*www.ideaguide.com*)

If you are interested in additional helpful and practical information to help plan or run any type of business, try visiting *The Idea Guide* Website. There you'll find practical tips, excellent information and helpful resources to assist you. Visit us at http://*www.ideaguide.com*

1 THE BUSINESS:

General Information on You and Your Idea

The first place to start when considering starting a business is to discuss *yourself*. After all, a small business is initially built on the skills and talents of one or a few individuals. In this first chapter you will discuss the following:

1A OWNERS

Identify details about yourself including any work experience, hobbies, personality traits, skills, talents, or education that would help you start and run your business idea.

1B DEVELOPMENTS TO DATE

Record preliminary thoughts, information, or events related to your business idea that have occurred since you began to consider it.

1A OWNERS: Who would eventually start the business?

This first section simply involves recording some basic information about yourself and the proposed business idea such as the type of business. Ideally, a business is started by experienced or knowledgeable individuals. Experience is not measured by age but rather by relevant expertise, training, education, or work experience. For example, someone considering starting a restaurant should demonstrate some basic knowledge of restaurant operations.

However, those lacking in practical work experience may have other skills, life experiences, talents, hobbies (the hobby itself could be the business idea), achievements, or training that would make them a valuable asset in a small business. Creativity, organizing skills, an outgoing personality, or skill with numbers are just a few examples of characteristics that each in their own way would contribute to the success of a small business. There is no set list of characteristics or personality traits that are more important than another set. In fact, it is difficult for one person to have all of the skills that help make a business successful. You may be able to find a willing partner, volunteer, or employee who can help with the basic knowledge of a product or service or lend their skills and personality traits to making it successful (finding these types of individuals will be discussed later). The most important ingredients are a belief in the idea and willingness and determination to improve it.

Example

Metal Works Fabricating will be started by Stuart and Samantha. Stuart is a skilled certified welder with six years experience in metal fabrication for the construction industry. He will handle all aspects of the manufacturing operations. Samantha will be the sales representative for the company, sourcing clients and discussing their fabrication needs. She has taken several sales training courses and has experience in sales.

Planning Questions 1A

1. Discuss very briefly what type of business you want to eventually start (or have started)?

- Retail candy store

2. Give a brief description of the proposed founders in terms of experience, training, education, skills, personality traits or talents they would bring to this type of business.

- 15 years retail experience (8 yrs management) food
- attended candy shows + siminars
- good people skills
- excellent product knowledge (consumer)
- Have worked in this area before - purchased + managed.

Evaluator's Thoughts

An evaluator of the idea would look to see if the proposed owners have any relevant experience, training, education, or talents to guide them. If it is not readily apparent, they would also be curious as to why the owner is interested in this type of business idea. When a person has an interest in starting a certain business (related to a hobby or skill) they are likely to be very committed to making it a success. For a business that has already been started, an evaluator would want to know how long and how successfully the business has been operating.

1B DEVELOPMENTS TO DATE: What have you accomplished so far?

This section enables you to keep track of any developments that have contributed to the development of your idea for a business. Much of what you have done to date may involve either reading a few articles or simply just thinking about it. Some individuals may have already found interested customers, employees, managers, suppliers, landlords, and so forth. Although it may not seem like it at present, anything you have done, however small it seems, will have pushed you one step closer to owning your own business.

Regardless of whether you are in the initial planning stages or have already started the business, the sections of the guide will assist you. As you gather more information in other chapters, you can keep updating this section to remind you of the progress you are making. For the questions below, those in the initial planning stage can focus on listing any information or preparation that has been discovered or undertaken so far. Businesses that are already established can include general details of their start-up, initial products, expansion, or growth of their customer base.

Example

Steven, a computer graphic artist, is starting Rainbow Computer Graphic Design in the spring of next year. Steven has made arrangements to work with three computer freelancers who have several years experience working on advertising, banking, and architectural projects. This arrangement will allow Steven to avoid costly employee overhead by using personnel only as needed on a project-by-project basis. It also allows him to promote the accomplishments of these freelancers when soliciting business for Rainbow in various industries.

Planning Questions 1B

1. Give a brief summary of some of the developments or events that have helped you gather more information or develop the idea for your business.

- market surveys
- Sourced suppliers
- Check to see what the competition has
- got tired of working for people that knew less than I
- trade shows
- researched Demographics of desired location

2. When was or when do you think your business could be started?

- when the desired location becomes available
- 6 month time period

3. If you are an established business what developments have occurred (such as customers, employees, or suppliers arranged)?

Evaluator's Thoughts

The evaluator is looking for how much preparation the owner has done. If the business is already established, the success or longevity would be considered. Developments to date give you and an evaluator a perspective of how near you are to starting. This section provides a quick snapshot of where the business stands.

2 THE PRODUCT/SERVICE:

Details Of Your Idea

The information in Chapter 2 will become the foundation of your plan to start a business. The rest of the chapters simply build step-by-step on this one. The following steps will be covered in this chapter:

2A PRODUCT/SERVICE DETAILS

Think about your idea and the features of it that will appeal to potential customers.

2B BASIC PERFORMANCE REQUIREMENTS

Identify what your product or service must be able to do for its user.

2C LEGAL ISSUES

Investigate whether your business idea requires any legal protection.

2A PRODUCT/SERVICE DETAILS: How would you describe your idea?

Nobody knows your business idea like you do. This section allows you to record some information about your idea to help you sort out exactly what it is and why someone would purchase it. The first step involves considering all of the *features* of your idea and the *benefits* that each feature would provide for a potential user. Features can be any of the following: what it can do, when it is offered, who performs it, what it looks like, what it is made of, and so on. The benefits of someone using the product or service could be that it saves time, provides warmth, improves appearance, or reduces the amount of effort (see the side box for examples of benefits). The example on this page demonstrates some features and benefits for a wool sweater.

EXAMPLES OF SOME PRODUCT OR SERVICE BENEFITS

• easy to use	• saves time
• stylish	• reliable
• saves money	• efficient
• convenient	• consistent
• good location	• durable
• prestige	• saves effort

Example

Sandra received several compliments on the handmade wool sweaters that she made for her friends. She decided to look into starting a business to sell the sweaters. She considered the features of the sweater and the benefit of each feature:

Features	Benefits
Made of wool	*Stays warm in all weather*
Made by hand	*High quality construction*
Made locally	*Helps local economy*
Various styles	*Variety of choice*

It is important to speak in terms of *benefits* because *features* on their own can mean very little to people. Remember back to a time when someone was demonstrating a product to you and began describing confusing gadgetry and features of it rather than simply telling you the benefits in plain simple words. Because we know our idea so well it is easy to get into the same trap and confuse people by communicating its features rather than the benefits. Only some people understand features, everyone understands benefits!

VARIOUS FEATURES AND THEIR BENEFITS

Feature	Benefit
Steel toe in a work boot	safety
Home delivery of a grocery service	convenience
Investment counseling of a financial planner	increased profit
A spray-on cleaner	ease of use
A store featuring bulk foods	saves money
Technical expertise at a hardware store	customer service

Benefits will *appeal* to a potential user who may *want* or *need* them. The strength of every business is based upon how well its product or service benefits will *appeal* to its customers' wants or needs. This is as equally true for a giant multinational, such as IBM, as it is for someone considering opening a small antique shop. Similarly, you probably came up with an idea because you believe it has appeal to somebody.

Answering the questions in this section will help you more clearly determine this potential appeal. The questions allow you to provide as much information as possible on the features of your idea and its potential benefits to customers. You can also include any evidence of your idea's potential by noting either your or another similar business' experiences, successes, or customer feedback. These can often be found in articles in the press. Appendix A **How to Gather Information** provides other sources to locate this type of information.

In addition, as you consider each of the features and benefits, be aware of the potential *weaknesses* of your idea. These could be things that the product or service cannot do, potential objections or problems from a customer's perspective, or simply things you have not thought about yet. To explain the importance of noting your idea's potential weaknesses, consider the wool sweater example. Each one of the features and its corresponding benefit reflects a strength of the product. Yet the warm, special wool used to make it could be very rare and extremely expensive, causing the final price of the sweater to be very high. The sweater-maker could defend this possible "weakness" by pointing out that the warmth and quality of the sweater are directly related to the rare costlier fabric, making the sweater worth its higher price. Being aware of any potential weaknesses in your idea will allow you to address them before they start to threaten the development of your idea. In other words, you can put out the fire before it even gets started.

This section is essential for all individual business owners, whether they own an existing business, are considering starting one, or are offering their services as a freelance or contract employee. Answers to the following questions will become the foundation for your business. For best results, they should be completed prior to completing the questions in the chapters that follow.

Example

Janet and Barbara want to start Family Value Restaurant. They both recognize the importance of maintaining a family budget and both possess years of experience making creative healthy meals. Their idea is a restaurant with a creative, reasonably priced menu near the main shopping area of town. They began to list their features and benefits. Reasonably priced food will benefit customers looking for value. Janet is very creative and will arrange seasonal promotions, another value benefit to customers. Their location will provide convenience. Their cooking experience will be a definite benefit to the palates of customers. The atmosphere provides a benefit of comfort to weary shoppers. The hours would be mid morning to 9 PM, a benefit of convenience to customers looking for either a late breakfast, lunch, or dinner.

Planning Questions 2A

1. Is your idea a product or service? What will it do? Who will it appeal to?

Store - Product
    Sell candy
    Everyone mostly ↓ 25

2. What are the features of it and how does each feature benefit a potential customer? List as many as you can in as many areas as possible?

FEATURES	BULK CANDY	Neighbour location	Ready made gifts
BENEFITS	Lower Price	Convience	Saves time
FEATURES	Strong Industry Background	Store Promotions	Fun + clean store
BENEFITS	Customer Service	Innovative	Repeat customer

3. What are its potential weaknesses? How can you overcome these weaknesses?

- Freshness - Small purchases
- low turnover - streamline inventory
- low customer traffic - promotions + sales + advertising
- competition, saturated market - new inventory + focus - diversify

4. As a demonstration of your type of product's effectiveness, do you have any evidence of the customer response to or sales success of it or other businesses offering this type of product. Outline them.

- Since I have had an interest many similar stores have opened.
- Customer Response Market surveys
- spoke to owners (competitors) about sales

5. What stage of development is the product in (i.e., idea, model, already started, etc.)?

- idea ++

Optional Questions 2A

NOTE: Some of the following questions may help you to further describe your idea.

1. Will it be sold to a customer once or repeatedly? How long does it last each time?

repeatedly
until its gone

2. Is the product used as a component of or with another product?

NO

3. Will your business or other businesses provide any related service for your product (such as after market service, help-line, repair, warranty, or maintenance)?

guaranteed Satisfaction

Evaluator's Thoughts

The evaluator begins with the features and benefits of the product to determine whether there is a realistic need or want for this type of product or service. Any perceived weaknesses should also have been addressed. If an individual discusses how great a business idea is, the first question that comes to an evaluator's mind is, "If it's so great, why isn't anyone else doing it?" Therefore, it helps to have proof of the need or want for the product in the form of articles, successful experiences of other businesses, or customer feedback. Furthermore, an evaluator may not understand the technical terms specific to your idea making it important to describe the product/service and its uses in simple, easy to understand terms, and ensuring to identify the benefits of using it. The evaluator is also curious about the stage that the business idea is in to give an indicator of how far away the business is from startup.

NOTE: The guide will begin to refer to your "idea" as a "product" since your ultimate goal is to potentially sell your idea in the form of a product or service. For those readers considering starting a business to perform a certain service, the word "product" will also refer to a service business. This is for the purpose of brevity. The word "service" can have several connotations or usages such as "servicing" and "customer service." Instead, "product" will be used for ease of reference. The steps for planning a business to sell products or perform services are essentially identical and the guide is intended for both.

2B BASIC PERFORMANCE REQUIREMENTS: What must your product do?

The last section discussed the importance of knowing your product's features and benefits to a potential customer. While a product can have numerous features and benefits, it usually must accomplish one *basic performance requirement* for a user. For example, a car seat for infants may have the following features (with corresponding benefits in parentheses): numerous gadgets to keep the baby occupied (improved concentration of driver), various decorative pattern schemes to complement any car interior (visually pleasing style), and a revolutionary design (increased comfort for infant). However, despite these numerous innovative features, the car seat has one important basic performance requirement. It *must* protect babies from potential injury in an auto mishap. Examples of basic performance requirements include accounting services performing accurately, television stations delivering entertaining programs, and coffee makers making good cups of coffee.

Your basic performance requirements are essential necessities or expectations that the product must possess or fulfill to even be considered by prospective customers. Outline your basic performance requirements and think about how you will ensure your product fulfills them. Some ways to ensure fulfillment include adherence to government requirements or safety standards, use of quality control checks, suppliers' guarantees, or collecting customer feedback.

Example

Brianna wanted to start up a company to make infant car seats called Baby "O" Baby Car Seat Company Inc. She recognized that consumers expect car seats for infants to meet rigid standards or they would not purchase them. Therefore a basic product requirement for the seat is its safety performance. Baby "O" Baby will ensure that only safety-approved materials are used in its construction. Performance tests are also completed to ensure that design, materials, and assembly are all of the highest standard. The design will also have the federal government's Certification of Safety, a requirement for any product used as a protective device.

Planning Questions 2B

1. What are the basic performance requirements of your product in the eyes of a potential user?

    - to sell a product that is fresh + clean in a fun setting
    - Selling what the customer wants
    - friendly + efficient service

2. How will you ensure that these basic performance requirements are met?

    - Good inventory control
    - Store surveys + questionaires
    - Knowledgable staff
    - Flexibility with suppliers

Evaluator's Thoughts

The evaluator will look to see that the basic performance requirement of the customer is recognized and not left unaddressed due to a preoccupation with the claimed features and benefits. In addition, any steps that have been taken to ensure that these requirements are met demonstrate that you are well-prepared. This section also helps clarify the exact purpose of the idea.

NOTE: The next section (2C) of this chapter discusses general legal issues such as choosing a company name and opening bank accounts. Issues such as forms of ownership (such as partnerships or corporations) and potential liability are discussed in Appendix D **Legal Considerations***. If you are considering opening a franchise or acquiring the exclusive rights to sell a product or service, you can also refer to this appendix. Those with product inventions, artistic creations, or new innovations should consider reading this appendix as it discusses trademarking a product name, patenting an idea, and copyrighting an artistic work.*

2C LEGAL ISSUES: Protecting your idea

Most geographical territories require that small businesses be registered with the government to begin operations. Your local bank branch can direct you to the proper office. You can register a company name even before you begin actual operations. This may help you gather valuable information from trade associations, government offices, and other sources. Psychologically, an early registration can also give you a sense of having a living, breathing business, thereby motivating you through your preparation period.

The one key element in creating a *trade name* (meaning business name) is to avoid giving the business a name that is similar to that of another existing business. A name that is too similar to an existing name could cause problems if the other business claims that customers are confused by the similarity and, in turn, that you are gaining unearned credibility by being associated with them. Accordingly, an individual would likely run into legal difficulties if they tried to use a version of a well-known name or a name similar to a local competitor. A name search on existing names can be done at the government office where you register, or for a minimal charge by a "name search" company listed in the Yellow Pages under this title.

Once your business name has been registered, you then have the option of opening a bank account. A bank statement may help you keep track of and pay for expenses you will incur during your preparation period (these expenses may be eligible to be claimed for tax purposes).

Planning Questions 2C

1. Have you thought of a business name? Are you planning on registering it at the appropriate government ministry? *Yes, yes.*

2. Discuss any business names, exclusive rights, patents, trademarks or other legal protections that are held or are to be arranged (refer to Appendix D **Legal Considerations**). Who will be arranging for these legal protections? In which geographical territories are these enforceable?

N/A.

Liability?
Food items (illness from product)

3. Referring to Appendix D, are there any special issues of liability or insurance requirements that must be considered by you or by the purchaser of the product? If so, what steps will you be taking?

Evaluator's Thoughts

The issue of arranging suitable legal protection, if required, helps to reduce the risks that competitors or customers will take advantage of legal loopholes. Minimizing competition translates into better potential profitability. Reducing the chances for customer liability also protects the long-term financial state of the business.

3 THE MARKET:

Finding Customers For Your Idea

In Chapter 2 you thought about the *feature*s and corresponding *benefits* of your business idea. Then the appeal of these *features* and especially *benefits* to a potential customer was discussed. This leads to Chapter 3 and the most common question asked by all entrepreneurs and every business large and small: "Is there a *market* for this product?" This involves evaluating the potential opportunities of and factors affecting the market that you want to reach.

Some people use the acronym "*SWOT*" to describe the type of evaluation you are doing in chapters 2 and 3. *SWOT* stands for Strengths, Weakness, Opportunities and Threats. *Strengths* and *weaknesses* of your idea were covered in Section 2A **Product/Service Details** and *opportunities* and *threats* facing your idea will be covered in Section 3E **Market Environment** and 3F **Future Trends.** If you run into this term in the future, you will know that it refers to these steps.

Each step in this chapter will build on the one before it and allow you to accomplish the objectives under the following titles:

3A TARGET MARKET

Use the benefits and features of your product established in Chapter 2 to describe a typical buyer.

3B MARKET AREA

Identify the geographic location or the physical boundaries of your potential market.

3C POTENTIAL MARKET SIZE

Determine an approximate amount of potential buyers for your product.

3D SPECIAL CONSIDERATIONS

Identify special considerations about your target market or geographic location.

3E MARKET ENVIRONMENT

Identify potential issues that could positively or negatively affect your target market.

3F FUTURE TRENDS

Consider how future developments could affect your target market.

3A TARGET MARKET: Who will buy your product?

Your business idea came about because you sensed that a product or service with certain types of features and benefits would appeal to the needs or wants of a certain type of customer. In chapter 2 the important features and benefits of your product were discussed and entered into the guide. Identifying the specific type of customer to whom your product would appeal is where this section begins.

Potential customers that will need or want what you are selling are probably in one or more of the following categories: consumers, institutions, government, or businesses. However, there are many different types of customers within each category, each with their own set of needs, wants, and buying habits. For example, breakfast cereals are purchased by many different types of consumers. However, a healthy breakfast cereal is not purchased by everyone, but rather by those that are health conscious individuals. Therefore, a healthy breakfast cereal appeals to those consumers wanting the benefit of a *nutritious* breakfast.

Similarly, it is possible to describe your potential consumer in even more specific terms than in the four broad categories above. Defining your customers more specifically is known as identifying your *target market*. For example, if your customers are businesses, they can be broken down into further targeted markets such as "oil processing companies", "medical supply companies", "catering companies", "administrative companies", and so forth. A retail craft store would target buyers of materials to make crafts.

Narrowing down or targeting your market into a more specific segment allows you to focus your resources and energies on meeting the needs of the target market rather than trying to meet the varying needs of different segments. If you have identified more than one target market, each may have their own particular characteristics or special needs requiring you to examine whether your product's benefits are entirely appropriate for all of them. Identifying potential buyers more specifically helps you to decide if your identified target market is large enough to support your business idea.

If your target customer is a business, family, or other entity, a key element to consider is which individual is the main decision-maker in the buying decision (such as a purchasing manager, parents, or a bookkeeper, as examples). If your target market is comprised of individual consumers, your definition of your target market should take into consideration issues such as age,

VARIOUS CONSUMER CHARACTERISTICS

- Age
- Purchasing patterns
- Attitudes
- Income level
- Education level
- Likes and dislikes

income level, education level, purchasing patterns (how much is bought and how often?), and how they perceive themselves or want to be perceived (conservative, rebellious, independent, healthy, etc.). Other examples of consumer characteristics are shown in the side box.

This type of descriptive information can be found using the research methods outlined in Appendix A **How To Gather Information**. Drawing on your experiences of shopping and seeing advertisements, you can begin to appreciate how all businesses try to specifically target their products at a certain segment of the population. This target market information will be used again in this chapter and in Chapters 4 and 5 when you discuss your potential competitors and marketing plans for your business.

Example

Diana wants to start Accessory Room, a clothing store for women. She has identified her target market as working females aged 18-35 living in the city and surrounding area. Diana believes that this target market requires clothes for weekend wear or casual office wear. She knows from her experience that these women are image conscious but sensitive to overpaying for clothes. Rather than having to update their complete wardrobe when fashions begin to change, these women are looking for accessories that can update their present clothes at a reasonable price. Accessory Room would, therefore, specialize in casual mid-priced clothing and accessories in order to appeal to the needs of this target market.

Planning Questions 3A

1. Given your product's features and benefits, can you more specifically identify your target market?

2. List some general characteristics of your target market (such as type of industry, size of business, volume purchased, buying habits, or other distinctive characteristics).

3. If your target market is made up of individuals, what is the typical customer's age, income level, education level, attitudes, likes, or dislikes? How do they perceive themselves or want to be perceived (image conscious, cost conscious, adventurous, conservative, individualistic, for example)?

4. What benefits do your target customers want when they purchase (value, style, or savings, for example)? Does your product deliver these benefits (Note: this question draws on information that you first considered in Section 2A **Product/Service Details**)?

BENEFIT DESIRED					
DOES PRODUCT DELIVER?	☐Yes ☐No	☐Yes ☐No	☐Yes ☐No	☐Yes ☐No	☐Yes ☐No

5. What do you think are factors in the buying decision for your target market (cost, delivery time, location, quality, etc.)? In what order are these buying factors prioritized? Who is the key decision-maker in the buying decision (purchasing manager, marketing manager, parents, etc.)?

6. Has anyone in your target market tried the product or a similar competitive product? Why? If they tried it, what did they think?

Evaluator's Thoughts

The evaluator will look to see if the business has defined its target market and communicated a realistic description of their target's needs or wants. Whether the product can satisfy these needs or wants is also considered. Careful attention is given to whether the business has identified its target market too broadly (too many different types of customers each with different needs and buying habits) making them difficult to serve, or too narrowly (not enough potential buyers).

3B MARKET AREA: Are your customers in a specific area?

In this section you will consider what *geographical area* of the market you will try to serve with your business (this section should not be confused with the physical location of your operation discussed in Section 6A **Location**). Defining a market area may be a key factor in revealing the potential of the idea. While the odd customer may be outside of this geographic area, generally the market territory can be defined. Usually a business tries to serve an area of the market that contains enough target buyers. For a retail store, the location of the market may be defined as geographic area within or around a city or town. If you are planning to serve a national market through sales agents, distributors, or mail order, then your market will be national. If you eventually plan on selling to other geographical territories, this expansion should be well planned since another market can have an entirely different set of competitors and buying habits. Reaching other areas is discussed in Section 5C **Distribution**.

Example

Elisa's Flower Shop will primarily service the west end of the city. This area encompasses a large residential population that is presently not served by any other florist.

Planning Questions 3B

1. What geographical area are you planning to focus on? Why did you choose it? Are there many potential customers fitting the description of your target market in this area?

2. Where are the future markets (another area of a city, regional, international, etc.) for your business? Why and when would you want to serve these new territories? How do these new territories differ from your present market and each other (if there is more than one new territory planned)?

Evaluator's Thoughts

The evaluator is trying to get a feel for how realistic it is for the business to serve the identified geographical territory. Another key issue addressed is whether there are enough potential buyers in that particular area. If the business has expansion plans, an evaluator is looking to see whether issues such as competition and marketing in these new areas have been considered. They will consider whether the company's plan for expansion is realistic or overly aggressive.

3C POTENTIAL MARKET SIZE: How many potential buyers are there?

In the previous two sections, you identified your target market and a potential market area that you are considering serving. For businesses focusing on serving a certain geographic territory, such as retail stores or service businesses, the next step is straightforward. Approximately how many members resembling the target market for your product are in this area? This may seem like an impossible question to answer, but there are several ways to piece together an answer. Although you do not need exact numbers, you can be well-prepared by using sources such as the ones that follow.

The first and most important source is your own common sense. You know who can best benefit from the idea. Are there enough of these types of buyers in your area? If you are relying on walk-in traffic, simply observing the area for half an hour, half a day, rush hour, or a few weekends can give you an idea of what type of people are located nearby. You could also talk to area merchants, some of whom might even be targeting the same type of market you are. City halls, libraries, and the federal postal service all offer statistics which may help. These statistics include the number of houses and apartments, average household income, and population of every area of a city or town. When planning to sell goods aimed at an upscale market, higher apartment rent, house prices, or store rent may tell you that one area has this type of clientele. Higher store rent on its own may also be an indicator of a higher amount of pedestrian traffic in an area. Pedestrian traffic can be an important factor for stores relying on walk-in business such as a coffee shop located in a busy business district.

If you are considering an area to sell business products and services, consult chambers of commerce, city halls, and regional governments for information on the number of businesses in each industry in a certain area. A library is also a good starting point to find this type of information, since a librarian knows how to access an extensive amount of information.

Example

Victoria wanted to sell homemade perfumes and soaps part-time. She believed that the items appeal to a target market that was predominantly female, 25-45 years of age, employed, with an income of at least $20,000. She knew that the open air market held downtown every Saturday and Sunday attracted many individuals resembling this target market. She purchased a booth and began selling her items. One year later, Victoria was ready to start her business full-time. She decided to locate Victoria's Perfume and Soap Company in the west end of the city near several other retail stores. The surrounding area is full of young families and Victoria feels it has many women fitting this description. City Hall information revealed that the area had 3000 households with an average household income of $35,000 per year.

For those planning to sell nationally, many of the points discussed in this section are relevant as well. Libraries have a wealth of information on the number of businesses in each industry, the number of people in every region, the buying habits of people according to censuses and other studies. You need only take information from these sources, make reasonable assumptions and then adjust them to your business idea. Also, distributors in other locations can assist you in understanding different geographical areas. Using distributors will be discussed in Chapter 5C **Distribution**.

SOURCES OF POTENTIAL MARKET SIZE CLUES

- Observation
- Area merchants
- Libraries
- Media articles
- Distributors
- Postal Service
- Real estate pricing
- Area rental prices
- City hall
- Potential customers
- Regional government
- Chamber of Commerce

Markets can also be expressed by the number of customers, households, businesses, and so on. Regardless of which measurement applies to you, it will eventually help if you can start to make reasonable assumptions about how much is spent by the market in total dollars on products like yours. Why? This will give you an idea of how many dollars are available in your target market and an indication of whether there would be potentially enough dollars available for you. The example below will give you an idea of how to estimate the value of a market. Notice also that the individual in the example makes conservative estimates to be sure of an adequate potential market for the business.

Example

Lloyd is a mechanic who wants to set up an auto repair shop in a town of 15,000 people. At the library, he sees that there are 5,000 households in town. He knows that most households in town have 2 cars. A librarian found him a census study that showed the national average per household is 1.5 cars. To be conservative, Lloyd started with 1 car per home. He knows from experience that cars need about 2 oil changes and 1 tune-up per year for a total of $100. Five thousand households with one car spending $100 per year creates a potential local market of $500,000 in sales. Using 1.5 cars creates a potential market of $750,000 in sales.

Demonstrating the potential size of a market gives you a good idea of its potential and also helps you to explain it better to others. Try to make note of any growth that you observe or read about. If your product is brand new and there is no information available or you just cannot find any numbers, there is no need to panic. Try to find articles or magazines related to your idea, your target market or geographical area. You can point to other companies, potential customers, consumer trends, or anything that supports your idea. Force yourself to substantiate in some way your beliefs that the market has good potential. The methods in Appendix A **How to Gather Information** can assist you.

Example

Paul wanted to begin Precision Enviro-Scape to be involved in soil testing and cleanup of environmental damage caused by inadequate storage facilities. He has defined the gas service station industry as a major target market, along with other industries. The initial focus will be on this target market due to local government legislation that specifically calls for the replacement of all underground metal gasoline storage tanks and cleanup of associated environmental damage to be done in the next three years. Therefore, the potential size for this target market is 400 service stations in the region. As sources, Paul has used magazine and newspaper articles containing information on the government legislation on gasoline storage. He has also used these sources to find other industries that could face similar requirements. These articles help show the good potential of Paul's business.

Planning Questions 3C

1. Given the geographic area you are considering, approximately how many potential buyers are there in your target market?

2. How often do you think the target buyers purchase and what price would they probably be willing to pay per usage of a product such as yours? How much is this per week, month, or year (use the measurement most appropriate for your business)?

3. Using your answers from 1 and 2 above, what is the approximate size of your total potential target market *per year* (# of potential buyers multiplied by amount spent *per year* by each target buyer)?

4. Do you think there will be much growth in your target market over the next 1-5 years? Why? Do you have any proof (studies, articles, etc.) to help demonstrate the growth potential?

Evaluator's Thoughts

The evaluator considers whether there is enough customers fitting the description of the target market existing in this area. On the other hand, if a large geographical area has been identified because the target market is spread out, can the business realistically reach enough of these distant target buyers? The evaluator looks to see if the claims of market potential have been substantiated with statistics or articles to make them realistic. Attached copies of sources are an excellent way to prove these facts.

3D   SPECIAL CONSIDERATIONS: Is anything unique about your market?

Part of your market may have cultural, regional, or seasonal characteristics that must be addressed by companies hoping to do business within it. Special characteristics can exist for different areas of the city, country, or world. A good way to discover this is to speak to various companies selling products to the market. If it is an area of the city, a simple walk down the streets speaking to merchants can help reveal its special characteristics. If you are considering new or foreign markets, local chambers of commerce can assist by informing you of other companies trying to gain access to the market; federal governments also offer studies of foreign markets, which are available through most libraries. Most foreign governments set up trade offices in other countries to offer information on exporting to their home market. They also offer listings of foreign companies who may perform a similar type of business to yours. If you are considering exporting, it may be to your advantage to find a foreign partner or distributor who knows the special characteristics a particular market and can help you sell into that market.

Example

The target market for Elmvale Night School is working individuals who only have limited time to take courses of interest. The market area surrounding the school has become increasingly populated by families from other countries. Instructors from these communities will be hired to teach some of the popular night courses, such as managing money and home renovation in their various languages. This will help the school gain access to this special portion of their target market. As a longer term goal the school will consider offering courses that are tailored to the new group's needs such as English-as-second-language courses which over the long-term can help create a larger market for all of the general interest courses of the school.

Planning Question 3D

1. Does the market have any special issues that must be considered? What are they? How will you help convince buyers in these special markets to buy your product?

Evaluator's Thoughts

The evaluator is interested in the initiative the business owner has taken to uncover any special characteristics which could help or hinder the business. Any research you undertake gives an indication of how prepared you are to perform in this special market.

3E MARKET ENVIRONMENT: What factors may affect your market?

The condition of your market can greatly affect your sales potential. Does your market have any factors affecting it like the government legislation affected the environmental cleanup company in the example in Section 3C **Potential Market Size**? General economic factors can also be a major factor on the potential market for a product. The most visible factor is the prevailing interest rate trend. If interest rates are starting to move upwards, chances are the government is beginning to try to lower *inflation* in the economy. This could impact your business in the following manner.

Increasing interest rates on loans and credit card debts make borrowing money more expensive for consumers. Therefore, consumers and businesses will likely make fewer purchases because increasing bank loan and credit card rates have actually made their purchases more expensive. At the same time, *saving* money becomes more attractive because higher interest rates are offered on savings accounts and investment certificates. When individuals spend less on purchases and save more, businesses sell less and are sometimes forced to lay off staff. Therefore, not only are fewer people now spending but fewer people are working and earning money to spend. People without

> **Good business owners are aware of non-business trends affecting their company.**

jobs usually spend as little as possible on extra items, which in turn, causes even less consumer spending. This reduction accomplishes the government's lower inflation objective because businesses will not raise prices (and will likely lower prices to entice buyers). Your concern is this: if fewer consumers are spending to buy products, will they buy *your* product?

A prolonged reduction in consumer spending can result in a *recession*. However, recessions do not necessarily mean trouble for all businesses. An example of a business that would be less affected would be a *necessity* like the only local grocery store in a town, since people still have to eat regardless of the economic climate. On the other hand, a slowdown in the economy can be devastating to *luxury* items such as jewellry.

SOME MARKET ENVIRONMENT FACTORS

- Social trends
- Number of companies
- Free trade
- Economic climate
- Environment
- Government regulation
- Licenses
- Government subsidies

Ironically, businesses that start during a recession sometimes fare better than others over the long-term since they are forced to keep expenses under control to ensure their profitability. When the economy improves they have a good chance of making large margins of profitability due to their conscious cost-control. Businesses starting during boom times sometimes ignore this wise practice because keeping expenses down does not seem to be an important issue when sales are booming. However, when the economy turns down and sales begin to drop, these latter businesses are sometimes unable to adjust their expense patterns and risk going out of business. To get an idea of the economic environment you are dealing with, check the business section of your local paper or ask your local librarian or bank for booklets on this type of information.

The *number of companies* that are involved in your market usually provides an indication as to whether the market is growing or declining. A relatively *stable market* would not have many new competitors and would offer most participants reasonable (though not always spectacular) profits. A *dynamic* or *changing market* is one that is undergoing tremendous growth or serious decline. An example of a rapidly changing market is the growing computer software market. One of the factors causing its rapid growth is the increase in the number of personal computers in homes. Another factor is that more and more businesses are automating their office processes, increasing the need for specialized software to perform these tasks.

Factors that influence your market environment can be found *inside* or *outside* the industry. An outside factor like government legislation can help or hurt a potential market by changing the rules, increasing taxation on consumers or businesses, financially subsidizing customers that are purchasing goods or businesses that are selling goods, prohibiting certain practices, and so forth. Examples of other outside factors include the environment, free trade, social trends, duties, or licenses. Any one of these factors could help you achieve success or could create obstacles. To be successful, business owners must remain aware of these factors because they can affect costs, customer demand, and a firm's general success. However, if you are not initially aware of any factors, use your own experiences as a consumer to note how your buying and spending habits have been affected in the past.

Example

The economic slowdown has meant a steady business for Sarah and Tom's Hill Valley Hardware outlet. They have both noticed that customers are doing their own renovation and repair work as it is more economical than buying a new home in an uncertain economic climate. The home repair section has experienced sales revenue growth of 20%, necessitating the expansion of the outlet.

Planning Questions 3E

1. List the factors inside or outside your market that affect the potential market for the business. What is the effect of each factor? What economic environment are you in right now (i.e., boom, recession, recovery)? How does the economic environment affect the sale of your product?

2. Generally speaking, is the number of businesses offering similar products changing or relatively stable? Why?

Evaluator's Thoughts

The evaluator is looking to see if all potential factors that could affect the performance of your business have been considered. This helps reduce the chances of any future surprises. Clear identification of factors demonstrates that you are a business owner who understands the business and is prepared for the issues that are present or could arise.

3F FUTURE TRENDS: What will happen to your market?

What are changing populations and attitudes doing to the future of your industry? In the future, will it be a growing market, relatively stable, or a declining one? What are some of the reasons for the future you see? Trends can reveal increasing acceptance of your product and can contribute to the strength of your business. They are often revealed by studying your target market's population.

Demographics refer to characteristics of a certain group of people. Demographics affect all businesses regardless of whether their customers are governments, institutions, businesses, or consumers. Why is this? Because *people* ultimately drive the need for products. Even if your customers are entities other than individuals (manufacturing companies, governments, etc.), these customers probably sell to or serve someone else who sells to or serves people. Therefore, things that influence a population's patterns, habits, and behaviors concern every business owner and entrepreneur.

The Idea Guide

Population patterns are constantly changing. For instance, in North America products geared toward an aging population such as pharmaceutical products will likely do very well over the next 30 years as the large number of "baby boomer" children born in the post-war period between 1945 and 1965 become middle-aged and beyond and need various medications. Aging populations also engage in gardening, fitness activities, travel, financial planning, purchasing retirement dwellings, and other activities that will provide excellent opportunities for new and existing businesses.

SAMPLE EVIDENCE TO SHOW FUTURE PROSPECTS OF A BUSINESS

Type of business	Proof
An environmental cleanup service	Relevant legislation requiring businesses to clean up
Nutrition advisor	Published studies showing concerns about eating habits
Adventure travel	Demonstrate the growth in travel to exotic destinations
Financial planning	Articles on growth of aging population and the need for planning

Some areas of a country or city have an abundance of people *under* 35 years of age. These people will be working, consuming products, needing places to live, and raising children of their own; consequently businesses that provide products and services geared to these activities will flourish. Looking at population trends offers many exciting potential opportunities for an entrepreneur.

Examples of changing *attitudes*: society's increasing attention to matters of health, safety, education, or environment. A way to address concerns about the future of your industry is to find related newspaper articles on the industry or the success of similar ventures. Articles reinforce the attractiveness of your idea's future market by demonstrating the wealth of opportunity that exists. Keep in mind, however, that if you are selling to another country or region, the trends may be very different.

Example

Angela was considering future trends affecting her idea for starting a fitness club for people over the age of forty. One major factor is the large number of aging individuals. Another is the increasing recognition of the importance of physical activity. She knows that study after study is beginning to point to the long-term benefits of exercise regardless of when an individual begins. Exercise and nutrition are proven methods of improving an individual's health, outlook, and energy levels even after the age of fifty (she found this statistic in an article in Physical Fitness World, Winter Issue). Providing an environment exclusively for this age group to use exercise equipment and facilities will encourage them to participate.

Planning Questions 3F

1. How are changing demographics, attitudes, trends, and consumer behavior affecting the market for your product? Do you have any proof of the trends? Is your target market growing, relatively stable, or declining? Why?

Evaluator's Thoughts

The evaluator looks for studies or articles that prove that any claims about trends, growth, attitudes, and so forth, are realistic. More importantly, careful consideration of the future and its implications reflects that you are a forward-thinking business owner.

4 THE COMPETITION:

Who Else Is Out There?

In Chapter 2, you discussed the features of your product or service and, in Chapter 3, you discussed potential customers to whom this product or service might appeal. An important part of developing or starting a business involves being aware of other businesses trying to reach the target market with products or services similar to yours. Being aware of how you are similar and/or different from your competitors can show you the potential for opportunity more clearly. It also contributes a substantial amount of momentum to your goals of starting and succeeding with a business. In this chapter you will accomplish the objectives under the following headings:

4A COMPETITORS

Identify any competitors who are selling a similar product or service to your target market.

4B COMPETITIVE ADVANTAGE

Identify ways to demonstrate that your business is better than these competitors.

4C COMPETITOR RESPONSE

Anticipate any response by a competitor that might occur when you achieve your initial success.

4D BARRIERS TO ENTRY

Identify any obstacles that may prevent you from starting or others from competing against you.

4E MARKET SHARE

Discuss the relative size of competitors.

4A COMPETITORS: Who else is going after your market?

Part of developing a successful business involves being aware of possible competitors and their products. Competitors are any businesses which can sell a product that accomplishes a similar type of result as yours; therefore, the features and benefits of a competitor's product can also appeal to your target market. The features can be similar to yours or completely different. Even if you find a competitor that does exactly what you do there is no need to worry. Remember that an inventor of a mousetrap is not necessarily the best person to oversee its development and success as a business. The Japanese did not invent automobiles, electronic products, or microwaves but developed better processes for producing and marketing these products in the 1970's and 80's. Similarly, you have

> *Studying the strengths and weaknesses of competitors is an important step in planning a business.*

an ideal situation if your business idea has been implemented by others. You have an opportunity to study their operations, marketing, delivery, and customer service, noting how to improve some or all of these areas. Note in the box below the different features of three businesses who all serve a target market requiring refrigerator repairs.

Perhaps no competition exists for your new invention. However, *substitutes* may still exist. A substitute is something that people can use instead of the product to achieve a similar result. For example, people can use public transportation, taxis, or a bicycle instead of a car.

BRIEF COMPARISON OF REFRIGERATOR REPAIR COMPETITORS

Name of Competitor	Location	Features	Benefits to Customers
• Action Fridge Team	• north of City	• quick response	• excellent service
• Joe's Repairs	• central	• very low prices	• money saving
• Diverse Appliances	• regional	• sell and fix many different appliances	• after-sale service

Example

Mel's Power Cleaning Machine is revolutionary in its ability to remove harsh stains that were once considered permanent. However, Mel realizes that there are substitutes, in the form of traditional household cleaners, mops, detergents, vinegars, and soap and water. These items have market acceptance despite requiring extensive physical effort and not performing effectively on all types of stains such as grease or ink.

This section helps you keep track of your competitors and may help you to recognize potential opportunities not being addressed by any other business. There are several ways to find information on competitors listed in the Appendix A **How To Gather Information**. If you can identify, as in Chapter 3 **THE MARKET**, a specific target market to focus on, you will likely face less direct competition. However, sometimes it helps to see what competitors are doing before fully deciding on your target market. You will be asked to fill in a table describing competitors who sell similar types of products or substitutes to your target market. You can then see how to remain *distinct* in some way from these competitors.

Planning Questions 4A

NOTE: A table has been set up on the page following Planning Questions 4A. This table is to help you answer the following questions on comparing the characteristics of your possible competitors or substitutes. The numbers of the questions correspond to the number of each column in the table. Use point form. Use of a table is an excellent way to concisely summarize your competition for an evaluator who may read your plan.

1. Who are the competitors, what is their competing product and how long have they been established? Is their longevity a factor with customers?

2. Describe as many relevant features of their competing product as possible (price, quality, service, what the product does, hours open, number of products, and so on). What are the benefits of each feature to the target customer (see also optional questions below)?

3. What benefits are most important to their customers?

4. Is the competitor directly targeting your target customer or is your target customer forced to purchase from the competition due to a lack of alternatives?

5. How does the target market customer perceive the competitor (experienced, good service, poor service, competent, expensive, out-dated, etc.)?

6. What amount of sales does each major competitor have (low, mid, high, actual amounts if available)? How profitable are they?

7. Do the competitors appear to be well-managed?

Optional Planning Questions 4A (re: Question #2 above)

•Are they pricing in the low, mid, or high range? What is their approximate selling price?

•Does the competition offer a wide range of services or a simple selection?

•Is their location a factor to their success or failure?

•How do their customers perceive their business? Why do customers buy from the competitor? What do they dislike about the competitor?

COMPETITOR COMPARISON

1. Name, Years in Business & Competing product	2. Features and Benefits	3. Key Customer Benefits	4. Directly Targeting Your Customer	5. Perception of Target Market	6. Sales Success	7. Management Competence
			☐ Yes ☐ No			
			☐ Yes ☐ No			
			☐ Yes ☐ No			
			☐ Yes ☐ No			

Evaluator's Thoughts

The evaluator looks to see if consideration has been given to how many competitors are presently selling to the target market. This allows you to evaluate the competition and your own capabilities relative to the competition. Little or no competition can mean your business is a great untapped opportunity. Conversely, it could mean that other businesses do not similarly sense a demand for that particular type of product. In either case, the reason for a lack of competition should be explained. Many different competitors can mean a growing market, or can signal that competitors are trying to differentiate themselves from other competitors and increase their appeal by offering different features and benefits.

4B COMPETITIVE ADVANTAGE: What makes your idea superior?

Now that you have thought about competitors and their product features in 4A, consider what feature and corresponding benefit of your product or business would be better than these other businesses (such as a less expensive price, better quality, faster delivery, better service, better skilled employees, or others). In Section 3A **Target Market**, you identified what your target customer requires. If you have a feature that provides a better benefit to the target market than a competitor, or the competitor does not have this type of feature and benefit, you have what is known as a *competitive advantage*. This term is very important to business success and will be referred to repeatedly in this guide. The feature and benefit that gives you a competitive advantage should be *maintainable* or *continual*. It does not necessarily have to be the lowest price since this may not be maintainable. Companies with low prices as their main focus may be easily displaced by the next firm offering a lower price. Many new firms try to compete on a low price-high quality combination which can be extremely confusing to customers. It is also difficult to make money since high quality products or services cost more to make or offer and necessitate a higher price as compensation. Generally, people will pay more for better quality.

Many businesses, in trying to be all things to all people, are nothing to anyone.

Example

Rachel and Richard are skilled carpenters who make beautiful wood furniture, bookcases, and cabinets. They knew there was a local market for their work and decided to open a shop, R&R Furniture. The pieces took them many long hours of work to make. Because they were competing against a department store that also carried wooden furniture, they decided to advertise that their prices were "rock bottom", their location convenient, and their furniture of "superior quality". People were confused by the ads thinking that R&R was a discount furniture store due to its emphasis on price. The handful of customers that did come in were amazed by the quality and detail of the pieces. R&R quickly realized that they were too preoccupied with trying to match all of the features of the competition instead of focusing on their own competitive advantage. They raised their prices to a level reflective of the furniture's quality and stressed their competitive advantage of limited edition pieces and fine quality craftsmanship. Soon people were coming from great distances to buy their work.

Do not worry if you are having trouble identifying a possible competitive advantage. Although it is preferable to have something better about your business that is readily apparent, it could take time to identify. Perhaps you will offer superior service or staff friendliness. As you will see in Chapter 5 **MARKETING PLAN**, various creative promotions that draw customers can also give you a competitive advantage over a competitor. If you are finding that your product features and benefits are similar to other competitors, perhaps the target market is large enough to sustain numerous competitors with no apparent advantages. An example is the success of numerous fast food outlets competing for the consumer wanting quick service and low-cost meals. However, it is best to try and find something about your business that cannot be duplicated by competitors.

The Idea Guide

A competitive advantage is different from the fundamental feature(s) of your product which was discussed in Section 2B **Basic Performance Requirement**. A *basic performance requirement* is something that the product must have in order to compete. All accounting service companies must be accurate, dry cleaners must dry clean well, and infant car seats must be safe if they hope to be successful. However, a *competitive advantage* is something about your product's or business' features and benefits that makes it *superior* to others. This is one of the reasons why customers will prefer to purchase from you. For the accounting service it might

COMPETITIVE ADVANTAGE EXAMPLES	
• Location	• Life expectancy
• Longevity	• Suppliers
• Pricing	• Labour cost control
• Product design	• Staff training
• Product quality	• Customer service
• Product variety	• Quality control
• Product performance	• Reliability
• Delivery	• Durability
• Technical expertise	• Ease-of-use
• Turn-around time	• Warranties, guarantees

be experience, for the dry cleaner it is location, and for infant seats, additional features that keep a baby occupied and content. Since this feature and its benefit will appeal to the target market, it will become the focus of your communication (marketing) to the target market.

As you can see from the above box of examples of competitive advantages, there are many possible ways for a business to set itself apart from the competition. However, a business that tries to emphasize too many of these features will confuse customers and waste time, effort, and money; it cannot be all things to all people. Many businesses, in trying to be all things to all people, are nothing to anyone. This is what initially happened to Rachel and Richard in the previous example. A well-focused business emphasizes one or two competitive advantages rather than all of its benefits. Try to choose only the features and corresponding benefits of your product that will appeal to a customer because they cannot be matched by the competition.

The final example shows a company that stresses only one or two advantages that their target customers require and their competition cannot offer. In the next chapters you will see how your competitive advantage will also become the focus of your marketing plan and entire operations.

Example

Trish's store, Trek Clothing, carries an exclusive clothing line known as Outwear which is targeted at serious outdoor people wanting superior durability and reliability in their clothing. Outwear is constructed from the best available materials to make them durable, rain proof, and superior to the competition. All materials from zippers to lining are constructed from the strongest fabric available that will allow for comfortable wear. Other stores carry a narrow range of medium-priced casual clothing but are focusing on the weekend hiker. In comparison, Trek Clothing will target the serious mountain climbing and hiking enthusiast who spends days or weeks in the outdoors. These individuals will pay a premium price to acquire this type of clothing, because it cannot be found anywhere else in the area.

Planning Questions 4B

1. Given the features and benefits of the competition identified in 4A, which of your key features and benefits could be a competitive advantage (in other words, which of your features provides a superior benefit or benefit that the competitor is unable to duplicate)? Use the table on the next page to help you examine your benefits.

YOUR FEATURE & ITS BENEFIT	COMPETITOR	COMPETITOR	COMPETITOR
	☐ worse ☐ better ☐ does not offer	☐ worse ☐ better ☐ does not offer	☐ worse ☐ better ☐ does not offer
	☐ worse ☐ better ☐ does not offer	☐ worse ☐ better ☐ does not offer	☐ worse ☐ better ☐ does not offer
	☐ worse ☐ better ☐ does not offer	☐ worse ☐ better ☐ does not offer	☐ worse ☐ better ☐ does not offer

2. Is there a demand for a product with your advantage? What proof do you have? Can you demonstrate your competitive advantage (through diagrams, videos, customer testimonials, results to date, etc.)?

3. Did you uncover any potential competitive advantages by observing competitors? If no advantage was found, do enough potential customers exist for your product if it is similar to competing products?

Evaluator's Thoughts

A competitive advantage should be determined as a result of reviewing the competition and should make sense given the target market. The evaluator also considers whether the business is focused on identifying its main competitive advantage(s) or unfocused (by identifying too many competitive features that it will stress). The evaluator would be impressed by any proof that your advantage is unique and desired by potential customers. The evaluator considers whether it is realistic that customers will want the product if none of its benefits are superior to those of competitors.

4C COMPETITOR RESPONSE: What will be the competition's reaction?

When a new business experiences success, chances are competitors will begin to notice. A typical reaction by established firms is to lower their prices, since they probably have a higher volume of sales and may accept making less per unit to try and retain their share of the market. Can you realistically convince customers to give your product a try if it is now more expensive due to a competitor's price reduction?

The *competitive advantage* you identified in Section 4B can be used to help in your response to competitors. Perhaps your service, warranty, or product support information is superior and customers are willing to pay extra despite a competitor's actions. If the competitor tries to *duplicate* your competitive advantage, then you might have to find a second factor that is superior to the duplicator. This could be a factor such as location that is not easily duplicated. If you are attempting to service a segment of the market being ignored by other businesses, you will minimize potential reaction.

Example

Tony started Royal City Pool Installation to be an exclusive distributor and installer of revolutionary energy-efficient Pool King swimming pools for his geographical area. Tony anticipates that competitors in the local pool installation industry will respond to his entry into the market by lowering the price of their pools in order to capture the comparison shopper. Tony will respond to this price reduction tactic by aggressively promoting the minimal ongoing maintenance costs associated with the Pool King's energy-efficient design versus traditional pools. As a result, consumers comparing on a long-term cost basis will observe that a Pool King is the better value long-term investment despite its higher initial selling price.

Planning Question 4C

1. If you have competition, what is likely to be your competitors' reaction to your entry into the market? What will be your counter response? If they duplicate your competitive advantage feature and benefit, are there other secondary factors with which you can maintain an advantage?

Evaluator's Thoughts

The evaluator looks to see that potential reactions from competitors have been considered. If a reaction is likely, the business should remain focused on its competitive advantage as its ideal defense. If the competitive advantage is duplicated, a second competitive advantage to fall back on is not required, but is recommended. If you can find a second competitive advantage, it will certainly be impressive evidence to support your claims that your product is superior.

4D BARRIERS TO ENTRY: What hurdles will everybody face?

Some individuals or their competitors are prevented from starting a business by major obstacles that cannot be easily overcome. These *barriers to entry* are obstacles keeping potential new entrants from gaining access to the market. High barriers imply difficulty for new entrants while low barriers are relatively easy to overcome. A grass cutting service business would have relatively *low* barriers because the only requirement for starting such a business is a lawn mower. In Section 4B **Competitive Advantage**, you have shown how your firm is different enough to limit direct competition for your product. In this section, you can add to your competitive advantage by showing how any new competitors will be limited from even starting by barriers. Barriers could also affect your entry into serving the market. Some examples of barriers are listed below and may apply to your type of business.

Barriers to entry are obstacles hindering new businesses from entering a market.

Exclusive rights are special contractual arrangements for selling a supplier's product line. This will mean that anyone desiring to purchase this product line must go through you, a tremendous advantage if the product is effective and awareness of it can be generated. If you have exclusive arrangements for the product, you have effectively shut out direct competitors. *Special skills or education* make competing difficult for new competitors. Is there a special skill or expertise that you possess that is extremely difficult for others to attain? A skilled glass blower may have apprenticed for many years to obtain the necessary skill to run this type of business. It would be difficult for anybody to start such a business and compete for this market. *Government legislation* may exclude certain businesses from competing for the market. Postal services in most countries are still the domain of the federal government. Couriers can compete for delivery of business mail but door-to-door residential mail delivery is usually controlled by the government. Government regulation may even be present at the city level. For example, a street vendor may have to apply for one of a limited number of city street permits. Therefore, competition is limited for vendors in some cities. The limited quantity of vendor permits is a barrier to entry for new vendors.

EXAMPLES OF BARRIERS TO ENTRY

BARRIER	EXAMPLE INDUSTRY
Exclusive rights...Clothing retailer, industrial products
Large expenditure for equipment........................Oil refinery, pulp and paper mill, television station
Government legislation..Radio station, charities
Special skills or training..Investment counselor, graphic design firm

Planning Questions 4D

1. What are the barriers to entry in your market? Are they high or low? Why is each one a barrier?

BARRIER	HIGH OR LOW	WHY?

2. How do you plan to erect or overcome any barriers?

Evaluator's Thoughts

The evaluator considers whether any of the barriers are substantial enough to be an obstacle to you in starting the type of business. Barriers that can be used to limit competition are considered an excellent contributor to business success.

4E MARKET SHARE: How many customers does each competitor have?

In Section 3C **Potential Market Size**, the importance of having an idea of the size of your potential market was discussed. Now that you have considered your competition, the question of market share will be discussed. *Market share* refers to the portion of the total market that each competitor controls. While exact calculations of market share are not necessary (but are excellent if you have them), you should have an indication of who your major competitors are and their relative size from largest to smallest. Share can be expressed as the number of (or percentage of) the total market population that each competitor approximately possesses. It could also be the percentage of the total dollars spent by the target market that each competitor receives. If you are planning to market nationally, these figures (total numbers of competitors, sales, or dollars spent) may be available from the resources you can locate by using Appendix A **How To Gather Information**. Knowing how your competitors stack up can help you see whose clients might be easier to take away.

Example

Kathryn, fluent in several languages, will start Translation International to specialize in translating business communications. She sees a growing potential target market due to increased international trade. According to local Chamber of Commerce statistics, there are over 200 firms exporting products at present to foreign markets. Currently, the local market leader is a large translations firm, Export Communication (whose office is located in another city), with 50 clients. These 50 clients translate into a 25% share of the entire potential market of 200 export firms in the city. A group of language professors at a nearby university possesses approximately 20 clients (10% share). Kathryn has an objective of obtaining 30 of the potential 200 clients in the first year (15% share). She intends to take several customers away from Export Communication through her closer proximity to the target market. Market share objectives are 40 clients (20% share) in Year 2 and 70 clients by Year 3 (35% share). Translation International intends to be the local market leader by Year 3.

Planning Question 4E

1. Rank your competitors from largest to smallest. What portion of the total market (i.e., market share or number of customers) does each control? What is a realistic market share for you to attain?

Evaluator's Thoughts

An evaluator is curious about the relative size of the competitors in terms of their control of the market. This helps them evaluate the strength of the competition and allows them to see how your business might fit in. If you are not sure of the actual share numbers, indicate at least whether each competitor is large or small.

CONCLUSION: PART 1

Results of the First 4 Steps

In the first section of the guide (Chapters 1 through 4), you noted the experiences, talents, and personality traits that would help you eventually turn your idea into a business. You then put the idea on paper with all of its features and benefits and looked a little closer at potential users of the product by establishing a target market profile. You added to all of this by beginning to take stock of any possible competitors and the features of their products. Looking at your competitors helped you think more clearly about how your idea is superior in some way to others.

Congratulations! You have now read and completed the four most important and difficult steps anyone faces when considering starting a business. The next phase of the guide simply uses this foundation to communicate your product or service idea to potential buyers and discusses issues in producing it and offering it to these buyers. If you did not complete all of the previous sections, do not worry. The next sections of the guide may help you to think of information that will fit into the areas that are incomplete.

Remember, planning and starting a business is a *process*. It does not have to be regimented or structured or done continuously for hours on end, but it does help if you build on the principles you have covered so far since everything else flows from them.

As you re-read a section of the guide, your notes, or even the local newspaper, you may decide that you want to change your target market, product, or even yourself by taking a course, reading other books, and so forth. Even a conversation with someone else can give you a valuable piece of information that you never would have thought of, or a new point of view to consider. When you think of something or hear something, jot it down somewhere in the guide and it will spark something else. You will be amazed at how bits of information such as these will shape and evolve your idea, so keep your eyes, ears, and mind open and your idea will get closer and closer to reality.

5 MARKETING PLAN:

Promoting Your Idea

This section uses three key points from Chapters 2, 3, and 4 to establish some marketing objectives for your idea. In Chapter 2 **THE PRODUCT/SERVICE**, you determined your *features* and *benefits* and used these in Chapter 3 **THE MARKET** to determine your *target market*. In Chapter 4 **THE COMPETITION**, your features and benefits were compared to those of the competition allowing you to see a possible competitive advantage. The next step is simple. You will consider ways to *communicate* the competitive advantage and other key features to the target market to persuade them to purchase your product. That is the main objective of a marketing plan. A marketing plan should be done at least on a yearly basis to allow you to continually review your marketing effectiveness.

You will likely hear some people refer to marketing as the "Four P's." If you have yet to hear this expression, it refers to four words that are key to marketing a business that coincidentally begin with the letter "P." You will have covered each of them once you finish this chapter. They are Product, Price, Promotion, and Place (or "distribution" which means getting your product to the customer).

When a marketing plan is created on its own, often a SWOT analysis is included as the first step (the acronym SWOT and the steps to completing one were explained at the beginning of Chapter 3 on page 11). A SWOT analysis gives those reading only the marketing plan a brief summary of the prospects facing the product. The following steps will be covered in this chapter:

5A MARKETING MESSAGE

Establish the communication objective of your marketing plan.

5B MARKETING MIX

Review various tactics to persuade customers to buy your product.

5C DISTRIBUTION

Find effective ways to get your product to the target customer.

5D MARKETING BUDGET

Calculate the preliminary cost of your particular marketing plan.

5E PRICING

Determine pricing that both reflects your features and appeals to the customer.

5F SALES OBJECTIVE

Consider some initial goals for sales of your product.

5A MARKETING MESSAGE: What message will persuade your market?

You completed most of the work for the marketing plan in Chapter 3 **THE MARKET**. This covered the analysis of the market showing its opportunities and threats. Now you will begin to establish the rest of the plan which focuses on reaching the intended target market to communicate the benefits of your product. A *marketing message* is simply what you will try to communicate with your marketing plan. You know the competitive advantage and key feature and benefit (the feature and benefit that are not necessarily a competitive advantage but are the most appealing of your other features and benefits) that will persuade your target market to purchase from you. Accordingly, these must become the focus of your marketing effort. In the example below, notice how the competitive advantage and one key feature/benefit are communicated. Other features and benefits such as customer service, cleanliness, pleasant atmosphere, and comfortable seating are *not* mentioned since they would just take away from the key benefits (variety of blends and convenience of location). Judge whether a competitive advantage alone (if you have one) is all your customers need to hear in your marketing.

Example

The marketing message to be communicated in a marketing plan by Tom and Jennifer's business, TJ's Specialty Coffee Shop, is the variety of its specialty coffee blends (competitive advantage) and the convenience of its location for its target market of working professionals and downtown shoppers (another key benefit). Its proximity to the downtown offices and shops will be a major factor in attracting this market. The variety of coffees and teas will attract shoppers and everyday patrons who want more than just the plain coffee available at other coffee shops.

Planning Question 5A

1. What marketing message must be communicated in *your* marketing plan?

Evaluator's Thoughts

The marketing plan must communicate a marketing message detailing the competitive advantage and any other key benefit(s) that would persuade the target market to purchase from you. The message should be clear and focused, providing the foundation for a plan to be built upon it.

5B MARKETING MIX: How will you promote your product ?

You have begun to consider the marketing message that you are trying to communicate. The main focus of this section will be to look at ways to communicate this message of competitive advantage and key benefit(s) so that potential customers will pay close attention to you. Although this section is longer than most, it is broken into smaller parts covering *advertising*, *sales promotion*, *personal selling*, *word-of-mouth*, *networking* and *publicity*. How should you communicate your advantages? Should you advertise to your target market in the local paper? Would a personal presentation be the most effective strategy? When these options are combined they will represent a *marketing mix*, a set of marketing methods that will provide the best results given your budget.

Elements of the marketing mix will be chosen based on how well and cost-effectively they can *reach* the decision-maker(s) and *persuade* them to purchase. Every member of a target market, whether a business, government department, institution, or family, has a decision-maker on issues related to the purchase of certain products. These are the individuals who will (once they are made aware by some form of marketing) see the advantage of buying your product and will be instrumental in initiating the decision-making process. In some cases, such as with individuals, your target market customer and decision-maker may be the same person.

Example

Madeleine wants to start a childrens' bookstore in a mall. She knows that parents make the decision to purchase books for children and so she is considering advertising in a local section of the paper geared toward adults. She will stress her competitive advantage of a wide selection of educational books to appeal to the parents' (decision-makers) desire to teach their children (target market).

Establishing a mental picture of your typical *target market decision-maker* may help you determine what methods of the marketing mix to use (advertising, publicity, etc.). Where does the potential buyer work? find information to do their job better? live? spend money? get news? shop? What activities do they engage in daily, weekly, or yearly? Questions like these may help you uncover effective methods to reach your customers, allowing you to effectively design a marketing mix. Other cost-effective and creative ways of marketing your product or service can be found by observing other businesses for ideas that you too could use in your marketing.

> **Marketing is effective when aimed at decision-makers.**

While shopping, note the effective ways that other companies communicate and convince customers to purchase. A car shopping example was used in the **Introduction: How to Use the Idea Guide.** In this example a warranty and an independent review of the car might be potential buying criteria for the car shopper. Likewise, these are both excellent methods to market a small business.

How could *you* possibly use a warranty and a review? Everyone who believes in their idea should be able to offer a warranty or satisfaction guarantee of their product or service performance to potential customers. If they do not believe enough in it to guarantee satisfaction, perhaps their business idea is not good enough yet to go forward. Independent reviews can be obtained by asking satisfied customers for their comments. A new small business owner may offer an initial customer a free or greatly discounted job in return for a glowing review of their work. This review, as in the car example, can be used to convince future potential customers to purchase. The car example is just one example of how your daily interactions will uncover ideas to improve your own idea. Keep your eyes, ears, and mind open for marketing ideas because they are all around you.

Planning Questions 5B

1. Who is the key decision-maker for your target customer (a certain occupation, a level of management, parent, purchasing manager, secretary, etc.)? How would the decision-maker normally receive information about a product like yours?

Now that you know *who* to reach, you have to figure out *how to reach them.* **Advertising** is one of the possible *methods* of the marketing mix and can be done through mediums such as newspapers, magazines, radio, directories, Yellow Pages, television, business cards, flyers, and billboards. However, advertising is not a necessity for every business. You need to decide if any of these mediums allow you to effectively reach your target buyer at an acceptable cost. Because there are so many different types of mediums each with their own style and audience, businesses have access to a variety of advertising options to target a specific customer. However, for small businesses, advertising can be more difficult since it can be expensive and challenging to use some of these options (especially television). Some less expensive alternatives are listed in the next box. The key to successful, cost-efficient advertising is to remain focused on trying to reach your target customer instead of as many people or businesses as possible. For example, a local firm would be unwise to advertise on a national television broadcast or magazine when all of its potential buyers are within their own city. Similarly, a company producing industrial equipment would certainly not be communicating their message effectively if they advertised in a fishing magazine or a consumer

LIMITED BUDGET ADVERTISING OPTIONS

- Newsletters or directories of other organizations
- Sharing ad space with another business
- Providing free product in return for ad space
- Yellow Pages
- Business cards
- Special editions pertaining to your product category

magazine with a million readers. They should instead advertise in an industrial equipment magazine that is read by the purchasing managers (decision-makers) of the market even though the magazine circulation might only be a fraction of the consumer magazine's. If your target market is difficult to focus on because it is a part of a larger general audience (and you lack the budget to reach this general audience), you may have to decide which consumers are more important to you or more likely to be persuaded to purchase. Then you can determine how to best reach this smaller group. People sometimes assume that advertising is the only route for reaching potential buyers. You may instead be able to avoid advertising entirely by use of other effective marketing methods described in this section.

Example

Patricia's business, Permanently Temporary, provides temporary personnel to area businesses. She has chosen to advertise in the Chamber of Commerce newsletter which goes out to many large and small businesses. As well, she advertised in an edition of a local paper that had a special edition on employment issues in the region. Her key decision-makers in her target market of businesses are owners (for small businesses) and personnel managers (for larger businesses). Located in a smaller city, she may not be able to use advertising to reach area personnel managers on an ongoing basis since there are no area magazines (other than expensive national ones) focused on personnel issues. She will instead focus on other effective marketing methods like personal selling to reach this target group with her marketing message.

Planning Questions 5B (Continued)

3. In Section 3A **Target Market** questions 2 and 3 you identified the general characteristics of your target market. Also, in Section 5B **Marketing Mix**, the importance of identifying a key decision-maker (purchasing manager, parent, secretaries, see 5B #1) within the target market was discussed. Based on this information and your answer to 5B #2, is the advertising medium (newspapers, magazines, billboards, Yellow Pages, etc.) an effective method to reach your target market?

4. If you plan to advertise, what message will you try to convey to your target market (keep in mind your competitive advantage, key features, and benefits identified in Section 5A **Marketing Message**)?

5. Do your competitors advertise and, if so, where? Which of their key features or benefits are conveyed in their ads? Why do you think advertising works or does not work well for them?

Sales promotion can be particularly effective since its objective is to sell *higher volumes of product* in *a shorter period of time* by offering a purchase *incentive* to consumers. This is the "act now" approach to marketing. Sales promotion generally leads to a quicker response than advertising since individuals see the cost benefits of buying now. It can also be used in conjunction with your competitive advantage. You can mention your competitive advantage and then offer a financial or other incentive to try your product through a promotion. Examples of sales promotion devices are free samples, free trial offers, or discounts (see box below for more sales promotion examples). Other ways not necessarily related to the product are contests or free gifts with purchase.

A *partner in a promotion* can have an effect on the number of customers you draw. This would involve finding another business who will provide your sales promotion information or your product to their clientele. Usually their clientele would be a similar target market to yours. For example, consider a youth sports camp looking for ways to reach prospective customers. The camp approaches a sports store as a partner and begins an arrangement so that when someone purchases from the sports store, they automatically receive a limited time offer to enroll in a youth sports camp. This arrangement is free since both businesses are benefit. As in most partnering promotions, an arrangement such as this allows the partner (sports store) to offer an incentive to its own customers (camp offer) at no charge to itself in return for distributing the offers. You have probably seen this in your own shopping experiences. Another growing trend is for companies to offer membership cards or "buyer clubs" which entitle preferred customers to discounts. These can be very effective in building *loyalty* of a customer.

TYPE OF SALES PROMOTIONS

- Demonstrations
- Free samples
- Money-refunded offers
- Opening day events
- Trade show appearances
- In-store promotions
- Membership cards
- Buyer clubs
- Coupons
- Limited time offers
- Discounts

There are several factors to consider before deciding on sales promotions as a part of your marketing mix. The first is *how much of an incentive to provide,* since a promotion will cost you money. For price incentives, a 10% price reduction offer (costing you 10% less revenue) costs less than a 15% price reduction but might not attract as many customers. On the other hand, a 40% off incentive could cost you too much when a 30% decrease would have attracted just as many people. Also, the *timing* of a promotion can greatly influence its effectiveness, as everyone has seen with "Back to School" promotions in late summer or early fall. The *duration* of a promotion should be long enough for people to take advantage of, but not so drawn out that it loses the "act immediately" message that is being conveyed. Finally, the *image* of the product may not fit with "act now" type of promotion. A rare antique store wants to avoid looking like a discount furniture warehouse and so some promotions (particularly price offer ones) may not be appropriate. A good evaluation is to draw on your own experiences as a consumer and consider the promotions you thought were clever for various products that you purchased.

Example

The marketing message of Janet and Barbara's Family Value Restaurant will communicate its competitive advantages of family value and family atmosphere to customers. Promotions will be used by the restaurant in several ways to achieve this. A meal card will be offered to diners. For each six meals they eat, the seventh will be free. This will create incentives for customers to come repeatedly to the restaurant. Other promotions will include a "Children Eat for Half-Price" night on Tuesdays to increase customer traffic on what is generally a slower day by attracting families with children. Free refills on coffee and soft drinks after 5 PM will also be offered so that customers can see the value of their dollar at the restaurant.

6. Given your type of product and the characteristics of both your target market in Section 3A **Target Market** and your key decision-maker (Section 5B), would *sales promotions* be an effective method to encourage purchase? Which promotions would work best (gifts, discounts, clubs, etc.)?

7. What types of sales promotion do your competitors use and how well do you think they work?

Evaluator's Thoughts

The evaluator considers whether sales promotion would be an effective part of the marketing mix for the business. If so, does the promotion give an appropriate incentive to purchase or does it offer too much (meaning lost potential revenue) or too little (too meager of an offer)? Also, the evaluator considers whether the business has remembered to stress its competitive advantage along with offering the promotion. You should first determine if promotions are appropriate for you and then demonstrate why certain ones would be better to show that you are focused in your marketing.

Networking, Referrals and Word-of-mouth Most new companies have limited budgets to spend on advertising and try to focus instead on marketing tactics that do not involve large cash outlays. This may include working together or "networking" with another company that produces a complementary product. An example: a pool installation company referring a landscaping business and vice versa. Their referral of each other's product helps them broaden their marketing at little cost. Similarly, you can benefit from another business referring you and return the gesture by suggesting their product to prospective customers where appropriate. This can help save a customer time in searching for a reputable company to complete a task, and allows you to provide "extra" in terms of customer service. These "alliances" or "networks" of two or more companies can also help you take on jobs that a larger company would normally be called upon to do. This is an extremely effective way for a small business with a small marketing budget to gain new customers.

> *Referral arrangements expand expand your marketing at no cost.*

If you take the time to call someone with a lead for their business, they will surely call you back to return the favor with a lead or a name of someone who can help you. Networking costs nothing and is one of the most effective ways for a small business to grow its sales.

An indirect way of using referrals is to keep a "before-after" record of your clients complete with photographs of work performed or letters with comments (to show to new prospective clients). Another way to encourage referrals is to reward the individual who provided them. However, the most convincing marketing method (and least expensive) of all is to get present customers to tell others about your business (called *word-of-mouth* marketing). Word-of-mouth results from providing excellent service and handling any customer dissatisfaction in a manner acceptable to the customer. Customers then feel almost obligated to send others your way. Keep in mind that poor service can result in negative word-of-mouth (studies have shown that satisfied customers tell two others about your business and dissatisfied customers will tell their story to twelve to fifteen!). Refer to the end of the **Marketing Mix** section for an example of a partial marketing plan that includes networking.

Planning Question 5B (Continued)

8. Would low cost ways of marketing such as referrals, networking, word-of-mouth be appropriate as part of your marketing plan? What would be some ways to use these methods?

Evaluator's Thoughts

This section helps to show the evaluator that you are making your limited dollars work harder by getting others to market for you. This is very impressive and will reflect on your abilities, initiative, and business sense.

Publicity is yet another inexpensive way to promote your company. Publicity can include contacting newspapers to do a story on your company, writing a column for a local paper or magazine, or donating product or services to charitable causes. These types of publicity are free advertising. However, it is far more credible to a potential customer than paid advertising you arrange through brochures, radio, or newspaper. One key issue to be aware of with publicity is that the story that appears will say volumes about you and your company. Be cautious in what you want revealed about your business or how you come across to an interviewer.

Publicity is free advertising.

Example

Cynthia has started a crafts store, Cynthia's Craft Company. She has approached the local community newspaper about writing a short column every month on making a seasonal craft. Readers of her column are obviously interested in crafts and, therefore, are ideal potential customers for Cynthia's store. Readers of the column believe that Cynthia must be a crafts expert and observe that her store is in the community. The column helps persuade them that the store has the necessary staff expertise and material required to make a variety of crafts.

Planning Question 5B (Continued)

9. How could you use publicity in marketing your business? Try to think of publicity that will reflect *positively* on the way you do business and demonstrate your expertise and/or marketing message.

Evaluator's Thoughts

Publicity is one of the most effective methods of marketing just behind customer word-of-mouth. Using it will show that you are aware of the importance, cost effectiveness, and the eventual financial reward of a good public image

---

Packaging can be an important method in the marketing mix to help a product stand out against other similar products. Luxury perfumes try to communicate an image with their packaging. Food products, from delicious desserts (an image of irresistibility) to generic canned goods (low cost), are another example of communicating by packaging. Packaging can also be crucial to communicating necessary instructions, weights and measurements, safety warnings, language translations, or nutritional information. Claims made on packages should be checked by a lawyer to determine whether they contravene any government legislation. Packaging can also refer to retail or service businesses in terms of uniforms, clean trucks, store atmosphere or design, or any other element that could add professionalism and image to the business.

Planning Question 5B (Continued)

10. If packaging is important to attract customers, how will yours stand out? Are there any labeling issues that must appear on your packaging?

Evaluator's Thoughts

Packaging can offer an important marketing edge over the competition as it is often the only thing that a prospective customer will see when comparing alternatives. Packaging applies to everything from your product to your stationery. If you have superior packaging or must convey information on your packaging, ensure that you discuss it as it gives an evaluator a chance to visualize your product or service. Photographs or computer renditions of your product packaging or store layout can help in this regard. Avoid sketching any drawings yourself.

Personal Selling Another method to persuade a prospective customer can be a personal sales presentation. Sales staff can present information to a prospective customer such as the product's uses, advantages, or pricing that will help convince the customer to purchase. Situations requiring some degree of personal selling are usually purchasing decisions that involve highly technical products, extremely large expenditures (such as equipment), products that will change the way a customer does business (like a computerized inventory system), or a substantial amount of service before the sale (such as a renovation or custom suit sale). A general rule is that the more analysis the product must go through by a potential buyer before a purchase

> **Personal selling is very effective when used with other marketing tactics.**

decision is made, the more likely an in-depth selling presentation is necessary. Personal selling can be used by itself or alongside other methods such as advertising, sales promotion, or word-of-mouth (all of which can generate some initial interest which a sales presentation can turn into a sale). Generally, when used with other methods, personal selling can be quite effective in convincing interested customers to purchase.

It is very important that your personal selling reflect your competitive advantage. Sales personnel must be able to communicate the benefits of this advantage clearly and concisely in terms that the customer can understand. However, this can be tricky if more than one individual has a say in the buying decision (for further discussion on decision-makers see the beginning of Section 5B). The salesperson must be insightful enough to address each individual's required benefits. For example, the purchasing manager may stress delivery time, the operations manager may want a feature of durability, and the vice president of finance may desire the lowest price possible. This would require an effective selling approach that would address all three different needs and still focus on the competitive advantage of your product.

There might be *sales agents* in your industry that will represent more than one product line or company in return for a commission. This can be an advantage for a new business since agents can often provide professional selling abilities and knowledge of the target market. They may have many prospective contacts who would be interested in buying. A disadvantage, however, is that your product might not get enough attention when grouped in with other products that an agent is trying to sell. Comparison of various agents can help you find one suitable to your particular needs.

Example

Scott's printing company, Print-o-Matic, will employ a sales representative to call on regional businesses. The highly technical nature of the actual printing and the other issues of photography and materials necessitate the hiring of a technically-versed salesperson. This person will be available to provide advice to companies on meeting their printing needs and maintaining an ongoing relationship. Therefore, personal selling will be the primary marketing tactic used. Some advertising in local business magazines will also be used to create initial awareness of the service and provide leads that can be turned into sales.

Planning Questions 5B (Continued)

11. Why will you require a personal sales presentation? Who do you think you would use to sell your product: yourself, sales representatives or sales agents? Why?

12. Describe what, if any, special training is required to sell your product or communicate your competitive advantages, and whether sales representatives with these skills can be found.

13. How does your competition sell its product? Is it effective? How does it compare to your selling plan?

Evaluator's Thoughts

The evaluator considers whether personal selling is key for a particular type of product and whether a business has reflected this importance by including or excluding it in the marketing plan. The evaluator considers whether personal selling will be used with other marketing tactics in the marketing mix. Combining personal selling with another method can increase the success of personal selling because it generally requires less effort to make a sale after another method has initially interested a customer. If only personal selling will be used, does the business have effective sales personnel (and enough personnel) to both generate interest *and* turn these leads into sales?

Example

Now that you have some ideas for marketing your product or service, put them together in a "mix" like the plan that follows.

Marketing Mix of Tony's Royal City Pool Installation (introduced in 4C **Competitor Response***):*

Marketing Message: To communicate the superior long-term value (competitive advantage) of the energy-efficient Pool King swimming pool to homeowners in the Royal City region looking for value in their swimming pool purchases (target-market).

NETWORKING Tony, the owner of Royal City, has decided not to use general newspaper advertising. Instead, he will be contacting landscaping firms in town to communicate Royal City's installation capabilities of energy-efficient pools. This could lead to referrals as landscaping firms are directly involved with homeowners on a daily basis. In fact, Royal City will complement the landscaper's efforts to fully service a homeowner's landscape needs. Tony will network with firms trying to reach customers with money to spend improving their residential property. A local landscaping firm, Pride Design, has already provided referrals.

PROMOTION Tony will contact a local radio station, newspaper, or a hardware store and offer to put in a free pool as part of a contest if the station, newspaper, or store sponsors the contest. This will automatically lead to the Royal City company name being publicized alongside the name of the promotion partner (on the radio, in the newspaper, or in the store). Since many people would be interested in a free swimming pool, the many contest entrants will be used to compile a prospective list of potential pool buyers. Royal Hardware has expressed preliminary interest in the concept. Royal City will also appear at the Home Improvement Show in March at the Memorial Community Centre and staff a booth to promote its capabilities to people thinking of adding to their homes.

PUBLICITY The local newspaper editor will be contacted regarding a story about pools that will appeal to readers of the Home & Garden section.

PERSONAL SALES A sales representative will respond to customer inquiries by visiting their premises to discuss various pool options.

Evaluator's Thoughts

The evaluator will analyze whether the methods in the marketing mix are effective in reaching the target customer and communicating the competitive advantages of the business. The use of methods that cost little or no money (such as networking and alliances) are extremely impressive in demonstrating your creativity as an owner and your appreciation for cost control.

5C DISTRIBUTION: How will you get the product to the customer?

Distribution is the route that a product takes on its way to the customer and may involve the assistance of other companies or individuals known as *distributors*. Businesses rely on distributors, dealers, retailers, or on methods such as mail order or automatic vending machines to get product to the customer. Some companies simply grant a license or franchise to other individuals who agree to produce, sell, or distribute the product in other territories or include it as a component to their own manufactured products. To decide on your distribution process, consider how you can best serve and expand your target market while balancing the costs involved.

Example

Jim started Full Plate of Salsa as a part-time business and began selling his jars of homemade salsa out of his home and at the local market. Soon, however, he was receiving more and more orders which convinced him that he had a good product. He now wanted to reach a wider market. However, he did not have the financial or personnel resources to accomplish this objective, and his schedule was getting filled just keeping up with orders he had. His solution was to hire the services of an area food distributor who would be paid on a per case basis. The distributor recognized the unique appeal of the salsa and through its knowledge of the grocery industry helped Jim expand his market by getting the salsa into other regional grocery stores. Although Jim now makes less money per case, he reaches a much wider market than he could on his own. The distributor handles all order-taking and delivery to the stores and Jim is able to keep his plate full with what he does best - making salsa.

Using a middleman such as a distributor or sales agent can help a small business overcome the financial barriers that keep it from reaching a wider market. Even large businesses use this method, as evidenced by the large car manufacturers using independent car dealers to sell automobiles to consumers. A middleman may also have customers to whom you could sell if you used their distributing services.

Knowing your competitive advantage and target customer's buying needs may also affect your distribution decisions. If your customer's habits include quick delivery requirements, requesting large quantities, or demanding delivery nationwide, your distribution process must be able to handle these needs. An auto parts outlet whose competitive advantage is its wide range of parts and speedy order delivery to its repair shop clientele must ensure that its distribution capability can provide quick delivery as promised.

Planning Questions 5C

1. How will you distribute your product to customers (distributors, dealers, agents, franchisees, retailers, direct to customers)? Does your competitive advantage or buyers' needs affect your distribution?

2. How does the competition distribute their products and is it effective?

Evaluator's Thoughts

A distribution process, if required, should be chosen based on various factors: its ability to expand your market, the cost of using it, its fit with the competitive advantage promised, and its acceptance by the customer as an appropriate method of making product available. It should allow you to reach a wider potential market than you could cost effectively reach alone.

5D MARKETING BUDGET: How much will you spend on promotion?

In Section 5B **Marketing Mix** and Section 5C **Distribution** you thought about various ways that might be used to market your particular product or service. As you were reading them, some may have seemed appropriate while others too expensive. Coming up with a budget to spend on marketing can help you identify marketing methods appropriate for your type of business. Marketing methods are not the only components of a marketing budget. Costs related to training a sales staff or the costs of a distributor should also be taken into account. Creating a marketing budget can be made easier by trying some of the following activities.

The Idea Guide

First and foremost, use *your own experience* as a consumer to help you think about effective methods that other businesses used to communicate their benefits to you. Your friends can help by relating their experiences. Observing how other similar businesses or competitors market themselves can help you see what might work best for you. Talking to other businesses with a similar target market to yours is an excellent way to help you allocate your financial resources into proven marketing methods. It can also help you avoid spending money on methods which may have been proven by others to work less effectively. Talking to printers, newspaper advertising departments and other advertising mediums can give you some feedback on the cost of certain forms of marketing. Libraries contain statistics on various business industries that allow you to see what a typical business like yours would spend on marketing. Also, Appendix A **How to Gather Information** contains some tips. A good way of deciding whether a marketing expenditure is worthwhile or not is to consider whether the number of sales you would have to generate to earn back the amount of the expenditure plus a profit is reasonable. This is known as evaluating your *payback*.

Smart small business owners start off by concentrating on networking (remember networking costs nothing) with other non-competing businesses who are trying to reach the same customer. Networking and forming alliances will inevitably produce leads to possible sales which in turn will lead to *word-of-mouth* or *referrals* (which also cost

> *Your consumer experiences can point to effective marketing methods.*

nothing). The resulting initial momentum can be achieved while minimizing expenses. Sometimes creative sales promotions can motivate the target market to buy initially. Personal selling done by the owner is another method which most small businesses rely on initially due to its low cost.

Eventually, you can ask your own customers how they found out about your business and can get them to provide clues on what methods work best. There is no right or wrong in choosing a method since it simply depends on what you think your customers would best respond to and what you can afford. Marketing plans and budgets should be reviewed periodically (preferably quarterly but at least yearly) to ensure your marketing methods are continually effective.

Example

Martin's Complete Garden Shop is targeting (as his main clientele) gardening homeowners who want a one-stop-shop for their gardening needs. There is a hardware store that targets homeowners for other types of products and he has learned from this store that it has not had much success with advertising in local community papers or on radio given the cost of ads. Therefore, Martin is concentrating on the following methods. He will only advertise in the spring. Spring sales promotions (discounts) will be offered in the ads on a limited-time basis. The ads will cost $2,000 but Martin feels that the spring rush of gardeners will more than pay back this money and help expose the store to a large group of potential long-term customers.

To determine the total cost for the sales promotions, Martin must include the cost of the sale price that he is foregoing by offering the discount. He thinks that the cost of the promotion will provide an eventual payback as he could gain many long-term customers as a result of the initial price discount. He will also offer a Green Thumb Club Card (customers who purchase nine plants get the tenth free) which will encourage customer loyalty by rewarding their patronage.

The rest of his marketing is free. Summer and fall seasonal promotions will be communicated on a sign outside the store (no cost involved) that will be seen by passersby. Martin has also asked different representatives of his various suppliers to come in to give tips to the public on various gardening topics to provide publicity for the store. These lectures will also be promoted on his large sign outside. He is relying on word-of-mouth to spread news about his wide selection and the lectures to attract more customers on a weekly basis. Martin is also thinking of approaching the local radio station about doing a two minute gardening tip. The radio station will likely be able and willing to carry the tip because its programming is aimed at a mature market to which gardening is likely to appeal. The gardening tip on radio will give Martin's Complete Garden Shop extra publicity.

Planning Question 5D

1. What marketing *methods* seem appropriate for your business? What other arrangements related to your marketing plan are necessary (distributor, sales staff training)? *When* will you use the methods, initially, eventually, or on an ongoing basis? *How much* would each of your identified methods in this chapter cost you per use and can you realistically generate enough sales by using the method? What is your *realistic budget* for each method? Is there a realistic eventual *payback* for the expenditure?

METHOD OR ARRANGEMENT	WHEN	COST PER USE	BUDGET per month	BUDGET per year	REALISTIC EVENTUAL PAYBACK?

Evaluator's Thoughts

The evaluator, after reviewing whether each marketing method chosen is appropriate for the product, will look at its cost versus its realistic *payback*. Payback can also take into account the *long-term awareness* that a particular method will generate (such as in the case with an opening day promotion where many people will just visit and not buy but have been made aware of the store for future purchases). Also, necessary expenditures such as training a sales staff do not necessarily turn instantly into sales but can mean long-term benefits to your business. If there is no money allocated to the marketing plan, the evaluator would try to determine how the company intends to get its message out to its potential target market and would assess the impact of that plan.

5E PRICING: How much can you charge?

The issue of "how much could I charge for this?" is a question all entrepreneurs ask themselves. The answer is a combination of a few readily-attainable facts. Basically, you will compare how your product performs versus the competition (which you have already done) and determine your own costs to produce or perform it.

In Section 4A, **Competitors**, you identified some of the features and benefits of your product versus the competition. This *comparison of features* helps you determine an appropriate price for the benefits you are providing. If your features provide innovative benefits never offered before or benefits that are superior to competitors, you may be able to price your product higher than the competition, since higher prices often represent superior or unmatched products. If you have low operating costs as your advantage, then you may offer a low price to signify value.

> *Premium pricing is often used when no competition exists.*

Some companies start out charging more (called *premium pricing*) if they are the only ones offering a desired product, with the intention of lowering the price when competitors are attracted to the target market. The first VCRs on the market were premium priced costing several thousand dollars. A risk of charging a premium price can be a customer backlash against your product when other less expensive alternatives are available - customers may perceive that you were previously taking advantage of them.

Some businesses charge the same as their competitors despite their superiority in order to gain the attention of the target customer. How much more would potential customers pay for your product to receive the benefits that you offer? It all depends on how superior you are to the competition and how great a benefit this is to the customer. Generally, the more *superior* the *benefit* is to existing available competitive products, the more the customer would be willing to pay. However, higher prices also make the customer *consider* very carefully whether they require the added benefits. This *price comparison* was also done previously in Section 4A **Competitors** where you were asked to compare the prices of your competitors' products. This will help you establish an idea of the price to charge for your own product. If you do not know their prices or are not sure, try and find out at least an approximate price. However, this process of feature and price comparison will not provide you with a final answer. You also need to consider *your costs* before settling on a price. Your own costs can be the missing link to finally deciding a price since your costs directly affect how much you need to charge to make a reasonable profit. Someone working out of their home may be willing to sell for less than a large competitor with twenty-five employees (however, try not to undercharge for your services just because your costs may be low; your benefit may be worth lots of money to a customer and you should be rewarded fairly for this). Consider all of your costs for producing the product or delivering the service. Your price must obviously cover these costs. In addition, you will have to consider other costs unrelated to the actual product such as rent or utilities (Section 6K **Cost of Operations**). After considering all costs, you will have a better idea of what exactly to charge. For those who are ready to move ahead, Section 8C **Break-even Analysis** will demonstrate a quick check to show how various prices would cover the costs of running your business.

PRICE AND FEATURE COMPARISON OF PIZZA COMPETITORS

COMPETITOR	PRICE	SOME FEATURES
Elegant Pizza	High end of market	• Variety of gourmet toppings • Restaurant seating
Mid-Brand Pizza	Mid range	• Many locations, free delivery • Discounts for multiple orders
Paper Thin Pizza	Low priced	• Limited toppings • Limited delivery area • Walk-in clientele

As a starting point use your features and benefits comparison among competitors done in your chart in Section 4A **Competitors** and Section **4B Competitive Advantage** to determine what price would be appropriate for your features and advantages. Then consider your own costs. Feel free to do informal surveys among target customers to discover how possible pricing options would be received. Pose as a customer of your competitors and ask them why they charge what they do. Ask other related businesses this same question. You might be surprised by what you hear. This pricing exercise will give you an appropriate starting point to establish your price even though it does not necessarily represent a final number. As you will see from the following example, setting a price sometimes involves making some reasonable assumptions about your customers and your costs. As you gather more information about all of your costs you will have a better idea of a price that both covers your costs and is appropriate for your product's benefits. The price you establish will eventually be a major component in the success of your product and your financial reward for having a good idea.

Example

Philip wanted to start a company called Lightcost Lighting. He saw an opportunity to distribute new energy-efficient lighting systems that would save thousands of dollars in electrical bills for apartment and office buildings. After informal chats with building managers, he realized that they would be very interested in his product due to rising utility costs. Competitors only offered basic lighting systems so Philip tried to determine how much more his price should be. He determined that a building that was 10 stories high would save approximately $15,000 ($1500 per floor) a year in electricity by using his lights. Although each project would be a different size he decided to use the $1500 per floor savings factor as his starting point.

Philip decided that, for the first year, he would simply contract out the installation of the lighting projects. Therefore, he would not require any of his own employees He estimated his cost to install lights for a typical floor was approximately $1000 to pay for an installation company's services ($700) and the material cost (lights $300). He felt that $2000 was a reasonable starting point for his price but wanted to think about his other costs (such as rent on his office space) and, secondly, whether he could charge even more than $2000 while he was the only one providing such a product. He finally decided to base his average price on $2500 per floor because he felt the extra $500 per floor would not dampen the interest of the *building owners and would certainly provide him with extra profit. Because all floors and jobs would be different (for which $2500 per floor would be inappropriate) he would also be prepared to make a margin similar to the one established here. He determined that a $1500 average profit when divided by his average sale price of $2500 results in an average 60% profit margin which he believes he can make on each job.*

Planning Question 5E

1. Given the features comparison completed in Section 4A **Competitors**, what is an appropriate price range for your product?

2. What is the price comparison among competitors at present? Does this correspond with their provided benefits? Given your answer to question 1 above, how much could you charge for yours?

	YOU	COMPETITOR	COMPETITOR	COMPETITOR
PRICE RANGE (low, medium, high or insert actual number)				
Corresponds with offered benefits (yes or no)				

3. How much do you think a potential target market customer would pay for the benefits that your product offers?

4. What cost do you incur directly to produce one unit of product or one order for your service (Note: you may require further reading before being able to calculate this figure. However, try to estimate an amount to allow yourself to think about prices you would need to charge)?

Evaluator's Thoughts

The evaluator will look to see that the price is realistic in that it corresponds with the compared benefits of the product and the competition. Circumstances of the individual owner (level of desired profit or costs) and the industry (like number of direct competitors or the superiority of the product) will also be noted in determining if the price is appropriate.

5F SALES OBJECTIVES: How much will you sell?

Most established businesses have an idea of how many sales they would like to (or have to) achieve since they have a history of sales and costs from which to derive a rough estimate. When you are considering starting a business, your lack of history makes it challenging to estimate a sales figure. However, using this guide has already provided you with many of the pieces to the answer. In Section 3A **Target Market** you described a *typical customer*. In Section 3C **Potential Market Size** you determined an approximate *number* of customers. A review of Chapter 3 **THE MARKET** can help you consider how many available buyers (and consequently, sales) there are and the nature of their buying habits (how often you can sell to them). In Section 4A **Competitors** you took into account how other businesses offering similar products were faring with their features and benefits. Section 4E **Market Share** asked you to consider attainable sales levels. You discussed and considered the effectiveness of various methods in Section 5B **Marketing Mix** and how they might communicate your competitive advantage, and in Section 5D **Marketing Budget**, the cost of these methods. Finally, in Section 5E **Pricing**, you considered an appropriate price that would help convince a customer to try your product. One other issue to consider is whether you would pursue your business full-time. Setting a sales objective may also involve using some of the methods outlined in the Appendix A **How to Gather Information.** If you do not have a sales objective yet, leave it and continue reading. Some of the upcoming steps may give you clues.

SALES LEVEL FACTORS

- Habits of Target Buyer
- Size of Market
- Competitive Advantage
- Price
- Marketing Mix
- State of the Economy

Example

Tom and Jennifer want to start TJ's Specialty Coffee Shop, as mentioned in Section 5A. They would target downtown professionals and shoppers. Based on the high amount of pedestrian traffic (they stood and counted a daily average of 700 people) and little competition in the area (one sit-down restaurant serving full meals), they feel they can charge a premium price for their specialty coffees and still attract the target market. Since coffee is not a well-planned purchase, it does not require extensive marketing communication. Instead, Tom and Jennifer will rely mostly on their store-front sign as the main method in their marketing mix. The sales objective is to achieve an average of $120 (an average of 65 people spending an average of $2.00 each) in sales per day for an approximate yearly total of $47,000.

Planning Questions 5F

1. Given the various factors mentioned above, what are your sales objectives for your target market in your first year? What are your reasons or assumptions? What about Year 2?

YEAR	# of ORDERS	PRICE	TOTAL REVENUE	REASONING
1				
2				

Evaluator's Thoughts

The evaluator wants to see that the sales objective is a realistic number given the factors of Target Market, Size of Market, Competition Comparison, Pricing, Marketing Mix and other opportunities or threats (described by several sections in Chapter 3) affecting the market. Any assumptions that you used to derive a sales figure also show that careful consideration went into the final number. Note that if you decide to present this marketing plan by itself or as part of a larger business plan, the **Sales Objectives** section above should be placed before **Marketing Message** at the beginning of the chapter. This will allow an evaluator to see your overall sales objective before reading the rest of the marketing plan. The evaluator can then better appreciate why you are using certain marketing methods.

6 BUSINESS OPERATIONS:

Running A Business

NOTE: Answers to the questions in this section should be general if you are in the initial stages of thinking about your idea. It may be premature at this stage of your planning process to furnish exact details of your operations. However, you should try and acquire a solid grasp of how these aspects can affect your business on a day-to-day basis. Some of the sections in this chapter such as inventory or environment may seem irrelevant to your type of business. Simply skip these sections and continue. However, keep in mind that the principles discussed in those sections can be applied to other areas of your business or may help you understand a competitor or supplier better.

Many businesses neglect proper operations planning, believing that success in business operations will follow automatically from product and marketing planning. Instead, operations planning must be included in the development of a business idea. It allows the business owner to efficiently produce and deliver the product or service and meet the target customer's needs in a consistent way. McDonald's promises its customers quick, tasty, cost-efficient meals in spotless surroundings. Accordingly, customers can go into any McDonald's restaurant in the world and these attributes are consistently evident, which keeps customers coming back for more. McDonald's success is not only due to its marketing but by thorough planning of its operations to appeal to customer needs.

Your customers are attracted by the combination of your **Competitive Advantage** (see Section 4B) and other key benefits they require. Operations planning should be pursued with the objective of supporting your competitive advantage when producing your product or delivering your service. For example, if your competitive advantage is having the best quality product or service, each aspect of your operations such as equipment, personnel, and suppliers must contribute to the quality of the item. To put it another way, your **MARKETING PLAN** in Chapter 5 is based on communicating the competitive advantage and key benefits that will appeal to your target market while your operations must make these features *possible*. These are the elements that will be discussed:

6A LOCATION

Consider your needs and those of your customers in reviewing a potential location.

6B SUPPLIERS

Determine ways to manage your type of suppliers effectively.

6C ORDER PROCESSING

Identify how you would handle orders and payment.

6D HANDLING AND DELIVERY

Identify any relevant issues in the movement of goods to the customer.

6E INVENTORY

Identify priority items to monitor that could maximize business revenue.

6F EQUIPMENT

Determine initial equipment requirements.

6G CAPACITY

Consider how much initial and future space you would require.

6H INFORMATION

Consider ways to stay on top of key areas of your business.

6I ENVIRONMENT

Identify any potential environmental risks facing you or your business.

6J KEY SUCCESS FACTORS

Identify the key issue(s) that will make your business a success.

6K COST OF OPERATIONS

Use the information in the chapter to determine any preliminary costs of operations.

6A LOCATION: Where will you locate?

For some businesses, location is the key element that supports their competitive advantage of convenience or customer service. The clearest example is retail outlets that rely on walk-in or drive-by traffic. For a service business, location could support an advantage of quick reaction time. Other reasons to pick a certain location are zoning regulation requirements, proximity to suppliers or transportation routes, and so forth. For other businesses, location is merely part of a company image (a retail store in an upscale shopping area). The key issue in choosing a location is balancing your requirements with the cost involved. Is it absolutely imperative to locate in a certain area, or can you move a small distance away and save money without diminishing the advantages of your product? This is the principle that many new business owners follow when they work out of home in the beginning to minimize cash outlay. With fax machines, computers, and sophisticated telephone services, the home business market is experiencing major growth. This could be an excellent route for you to initially start your business on a full or part-time basis.

> *Operations must focus on supporting your competitive advantage.*

Example

Michael had worked as an operations supervisor in an automobile manufacturing plant. While working there, he observed that pre-assembly of certain parts would save the car company money. He decided to look into starting his own company to do this pre-assembly. He knew from experience that he needed to locate at most an hour's drive or closer from the car plants to offer them the reliability and quick response that they demanded from all suppliers. This demand is made because the car plants do not want to carry large amounts of parts inventory, due to their cost, but also cannot sit idle waiting for parts delivery. Therefore, it is crucial for suppliers like Michael to help in this objective by reacting quickly to orders.

Planning Questions 6A

1. Identify where you are considering locating and the reasons why you would locate your operations there. If location is relevant to customers' needs, do these locations address them?

Evaluator's Thoughts

The evaluator wants to the see that a business has considered the implications of its location choice in terms of impact on competitive advantage, customer requirements, and cost. If you can minimize your location costs (as is possible with a non-retail situation) while still providing the promised features, benefits, and competitive advantage, you are well-positioned for profitable results.

6B SUPPLIERS: Who will provide you with key items and services?

Suppliers play a key role in helping you service your customers and they can come in many different forms. Suppliers can provide their services as in the case of an interior designer who requires tradespeople to implement a design. Other suppliers provide retail stores or other businesses with actual items for eventual resale. In fact, your idea might involve being a supplier to someone else. Just as you are eager to gain business, suppliers are eager to gain *your* business. Locating as many alternative sources of supply as possible creates competition among suppliers and allows you to benefit from better pricing and service. However, you can also benefit by establishing a good long-term relationship with a reliable supplier. A reliable supplier providing excellent service can make it seem like you have a partner helping you achieve your objectives.

A small business can monitor and manage suppliers much easier than a large manufacturing company that must purchase hundreds of components or raw materials from hundreds of different suppliers. However, both have similar purchasing considerations. Both must be able to count on *reliable* suppliers

> ## Good relationships with suppliers can make it seem like you have a partner.

who can continually provide products or services. Both need to avoid being forced to *purchase unnecessary quantities* from suppliers, which can tie up valuable cash in raw materials or products that move less quickly. Small and large businesses both need to be aware of *lead times* (the time required to receive items from a supplier once the order is placed) and how lead times can affect timely fulfillment of customer orders. Also, the *terms of payment* (period of time allowed by a supplier for payment) can be very important since both large and small businesses might not be paid immediately upon selling their own products (and so should avoid having to pay suppliers too soon). An appropriate analogy is being forced to pay household bills before receiving your bi-weekly pay. These considerations must finally be balanced by considering the *prices* and *service* of a supplier. Having alternative suppliers helps you address these main purchasing concerns.

Example

Maria and Hugh were deciding on products to sell in a mail-order catalog business they were considering. Before they settled on all of the products they would offer, they needed to study several things. They needed to know that each supplier would be reliable since their ads promised customers convenient shopping at home with quick delivery of product in 5 days. In addition, the product had to be reasonably priced for customers yet allow Hugh and Maria to make a profit once shipping and handling, postage, and other costs were factored in.

Several suppliers offered them better deals if they bought larger amounts. However, they realized that this would be a large initial expense and they might get stuck with large quantities of unsold merchandise. Furthermore, suppliers wanted to be paid right away since Maria and Hugh were a new business.

Given all the considerations, Hugh and Maria realized one key thing: they had many interested suppliers, so they began to use their bargaining leverage. They offered to choose one exclusive supplier for each product. This created incentive for suppliers to begin cooperating since each supplier knew they had a chance at large amounts of repeat sales if their product was popular with Hugh and Maria's customers. However, in return for this exclusivity, Hugh and Maria wanted to purchase less quantity per order to avoid the costs of carrying inventory, and wanted better pricing, longer terms of payment, and shorter lead times despite these smaller purchases. As a demonstration of their commitment they would pay for the entire initial order quantity in cash. Several suppliers agreed and Hugh and Maria garnered some key long-term benefits that will help make their business a success.

Planning Questions 6B

1. What type of suppliers do you require? Have you identified any potential candidates or made arrangements with any suppliers for each requirement?

2. Do you have supplier alternatives? How will this affect price, service, reliability, and terms of payment? How will you prepare yourself if there are no other alternatives?

Evaluator's Thoughts

An evaluator wants to see that implications of the use of suppliers have been considered. Identification of alternative suppliers shows that you have some bargaining power with your suppliers. However, solid relationships with suppliers is also important. Just addressing the issue of suppliers shows that your insight is beyond that of most business people. If there are no alternatives, the evaluator would be interested in your plans to ensure supply is not potentially at risk of being stopped or interrupted.

6C ORDER PROCESSING: How will you handle an order?

People start businesses to receive orders. It is important to carefully plan how orders are handled to ensure that customers wanting to purchase are not turned off once they have made a decision to do so. Some companies prioritize certain orders to meet the needs of their valued clients. Rush orders are also a consideration since they can impact other elements of operations. Patterns will likely occur once you begin; perhaps 20% of your customers will provide a large portion of your sales. Likely, you will tailor your handling of orders to better service these customers.

The accuracy and efficiency of billing is crucial to receiving the *correct* amount of money *on time*. Any delays in issuing bills cause delays in collecting money owed to you *(account receivables)*. This can strain a company's cash flow and translate into a shortage of cash or higher usage of a credit line than necessary (see Section 8B **Cash Flow Statement**). Perhaps you may need to offer a discount to encourage early payment, a common business practice. Occasionally, you see items such as "2/10, n30" on a bill. This means that the business is offering an incentive to pay early through a 2% discount if it receives payment in 10 days. Otherwise, the "net" amount (entire amount) is due in 30 days.

Waiting might be a daily part of doing business if your customers are large enough that they pay only when they want to. Businesses generally offer payment terms of 30, 45, or 60 days after purchase to their business customers but sometimes larger companies do not pay until 90 days or more have passed. You just need to anticipate whether customers are responsible enough to be granted credit and you will be fine. Any signs of financial difficulty in a customer or a lack of knowledge about who they are should be investigated through your bank. This can be done by asking your bank to do a credit check on the potential client. Some businesses require the first purchase to be made in cash before granting credit to an unknown customer.

Planning Questions 6C

1. Give a step-by-step description of how an order is handled, from actual sale to collection of money. How long does this take? Are there any other considerations (credit check, rush orders, order priority) you might have to make?

2. How are customers billed (monthly, per usage, per purchase)? How will customers pay (cash, credit card, on account with a certain term of days until due)? How many days will it take to receive the payment?

Evaluator's Thoughts

This crucial aspect of operations is largely ignored by both large and small businesses. The results of good preparation are very financially rewarding, while a lack of acknowledgment of the order processing and collection issue can be equally disastrous. Show you are well-prepared by discussing your process, particularly the length of time you will need to wait to get paid.

6D HANDLING AND DELIVERY: How do you get product to a customer?

The way your business delivers sold goods can have a large impact on your pricing, level of service provided to customers, your delivery time, and the condition of goods on arrival. There are several potential issues. These include direct transportation costs such as fuel, trucks, drivers, freighting and other issues such as taxes, mailing costs, tariffs, duties, foreign currency exchange, or import/export procedures. Handling and delivery needs may also necessitate equipment purchases.

Example

Lorraine's Handmade Books has taken off in sales. However a portion of her market is overseas. Customs clearance costs, postage, tax issues, and exchange rate fluctuations have necessitated price hikes to cover her costs and delays in delivery dates to foreign customers. She has now hired a customs broker who can handle these related border crossing issues. Lorraine has had to consider these issues in her plan (after the fact) by including all of these unexpected costs and broker's fees into her revised financial projections. In addition to the extra costs, Lorraine may have lost several customers due to the border crossing delays as they may now perceive her business as disorganized or unreliable.

Planning Questions 6D

1. How will goods be moved to you or from you? Identify any specific required equipment purchases to assist in the transport of goods.

2. How do handling issues such as taxes, exchange rates, duties, or mailing costs affect your type of business?

6E INVENTORY: How much must you carry?

The goods that you have available will be a major factor in achieving sales. Changes in fashion, styles, seasons, and technology must be monitored carefully to ensure that you are in tune with your customers' needs. You may eventually be able to detect patterns in your operations. For example, perhaps only 20% of the inventory you are thinking of carrying will be constantly in demand, yet will make up 80% of your sales. This "20/80 rule" is a common business formula. In this case, it would be wise to spend extra to maintain sufficient inventory in these items and not invest too much money purchasing large quantities of the rest. Hugh and Maria in the Section 6B **Suppliers** example knew that carrying too much inventory would be costly since it might move slowly (large amounts of money paid out for each quantity but only small amounts trickling in from customer orders). Even if they received long terms of time over which to pay, they might not have the inventory sold by the time the bill was due. Keeping inventory at lower levels reduces the financing cost for a company and allows for better use of cash elsewhere. However, in the beginning you will have to rely on your knowledge of what appeals to your target market to decide on items to initially carry. Suppliers can assist because they may know what goods other businesses have been successful at selling.

Your inventory handling can also allow you to achieve your **Competitive Advantage** identified in Section 4B. Some companies have an advantage or key feature of low prices, so they try to keep inventory costs low to help meet the target customer's price expectations. Often this means lower stock levels and the risk of *stockouts* (when a business runs out of stock), a risk which customers may accept due to the low prices. However, low inventory levels can be disastrous if your marketing is based on promising customers immediate availability of products (or wide variety of products) like the mail-order example. Think of the customers that Hugh and Maria would lose if they ran out of certain mail-order stock. You must make arrangements for your inventory so that it supports your marketing message (which, in turn, communicates your competitive advantage and key features). For example, consider a business that communicates convenience (competitive advantage)

Evaluator's nightmare: companies carrying too much inventory.

and guaranteed availability (key feature) over a wide selection of items as its marketing message. To support this offer, the business will probably have to carry a wide selection of stock rather than large volumes of any one item. Buying only small quantities of each product, in turn, costs the business more per unit (since suppliers are unlikely to offer good unit prices if only a few are bought at once). The business must then set higher prices to compensate. However, customers are still willing to purchase because of the convenience and product availability. An example of this type of scenario is convenience stores which usually carry a wide selection of higher priced items. A solution for keeping customers happy while minimizing your inventory costs may involve working with your supplier to establish acceptable lead times to replenish your inventory. Shorter lead times both minimize the risk of stocking out and allow you to carry less. First determining your customers' needs is crucial.

Not only do high inventory levels cost more, they can also create risk of inventory *obsolescence* (products out of date, out of style, or no longer functional). Excessively high inventory can frighten off potential financiers because when a financier lends money to buy inventory (taking the inventory itself as collateral), they know they would only recapture at most 20% of the value of an inventoried item if forced to foreclose a business and sell off the inventoried items. This is why "Going Out of Business" or bankruptcy sales have such good prices. A financier has usually taken control of the items because the retailer or manufacturer could not meet its loan obligations. The financier must try and convince buyers to come in to quickly buy in order to recoup some of the loan money. You should also consider any issues that are important in the storage of goods (such as spoilage, space requirements, safe handling, or insurance) and how you will ensure they are considered in your business operations.

Example

After starting the mail-order business, Hugh and Maria realized that certain items were selling much better than others. Many of these fast-moving items were inexpensive and the profits minimal but the volume of sales was good enough to provide substantial income. On the other hand, some of the slower selling, more expensive items provided good profit when sold and they were reluctant to discontinue carrying these entirely. They decided to keep on hand a large portion of the inexpensive fast-selling items. For the slower selling items, they received assurances from the supplier that they could be delivered in 6 days after a request. Therefore, they kept just enough expensive slow-moving items to meet the expected demand for the week. They would also reorder what they needed for the next week six days in advance. This helped them keep cash in the bank instead of being in debt to suppliers for large quantities of expensive products.

Planning Questions 6E

1. How will your inventory handling allow your business to achieve its competitive advantage?

2. What inventory items make up the largest percentage of sales? Outline how you will ensure that these items are never out of stock and how you will minimize the unnecessary costs of carrying the rest. How can your suppliers help you manage your inventory more efficiently? What else can help you manage inventory (easy-to-predict customer volume requirements, inventory monitoring systems)?

3. Where will you store your goods? What is important in storing the goods (temperature, safety, insurance)? Why?

Evaluator's Thoughts

The inventory issue is crucial in helping the company achieve its marketing and sales objectives. Consideration must also be given to the cost of carrying the inventory. Any planning done to prioritize inventory into popular and less popular items, or finding accommodating suppliers who can alleviate any potential inventory strain, shows you are well-prepared and aware of the benefits of efficient inventory handling.

6F EQUIPMENT: What equipment requirements will you have?

Now that you have considered various areas of your operations, you can determine any equipment requirements. Despite their efficiency, equipment purchases at startup can be an expensive undertaking. It is extremely wise to evaluate your options before investing in equipment since changes could occur in business volume, location, or customer preferences that could render the equipment less useful. Some businesses rent before investing in expensive equipment. This enables them to evaluate whether the business volume is worth the investment. Computers are the usual first choice of many businesses because they can be used for word processing, maintenance of financial information, inventory information, and so on. Depending on the nature of your operations you may also require vehicles, production machines, furniture or fixtures (in the case of retail stores). Much of this equipment can be purchased used from auctions usually announced in the business section of the newspaper or by calling "liquidators" listed in the Yellow Pages. Used equipment may be a viable alternative for businesses not requiring state-of-the-art purchases. No matter what you are buying, keep in mind that your equipment purchases should be based on a realistic expectation of your business volume.

Planning Questions 6F

1. What are your initial equipment requirements? If the equipment is very expensive, are there alternatives? What will you need in the future?

Evaluator's Thoughts

Equipment is often necessary for businesses to be efficient in their operations. However, startups sometimes overestimate their needs and purchase equipment that is far more expensive than what they actually could get by with. This purchase can then become a cost burden if the business volume is less than expected. Identify your reasoning for needing certain equipment.

6G CAPACITY: How much business can you handle?

Considering all aspects of your operations gives you an indication of the amount of business you could handle, commonly referred to as your *capacity*. Considering your initial capacity allows you to make preparations for the future. If your business were to be immediately successful and sales were to increase dramatically, your initial capacity to handle the increase can become strained (location too small, equipment too slow). Therefore, it helps to retain flexibility in your operations to allow you to adapt to new circumstances. Examples include avoiding the purchase of inadequate equipment(see Section 6F **Equipment**), managing your suppliers effectively as discussed in Section 6B **Suppliers**, or avoiding unnecessarily long-term leases on locations in case you need to move to a larger space (Section 6A **Location**). Changing your capacity could involve acquiring more telephone lines, hiring more personnel, or making more machinery purchases. This is a nice problem to have but expansion should proceed carefully. Business owners often fall into the trap of thinking they need large premises because the growth will not stop or for reasons of prestige. Sometimes it is better to subcontract extra short-term work to competent businesses or individuals rather than invest in new equipment, space, or personnel, which could be a cost burden if your business were to slow back down. You could also rent space or equipment for short-term needs, or temporarily add another shift of employees. In all cases, future plans for capacity expansion should be carefully evaluated and supported by valid reasons.

Example

Christina, a self-employed architect, works out of the basement studio in her house. At one point, she was extremely busy and had to take on extra help. At first she thought about leasing office space for her growing business because her two new employees would be cramped into her studio resulting in less than optimal working conditions. Instead, Christina suggested that they all meet once a week to go over the project drawings. The employees, both skilled architectural graduates, could then go home after these meetings and use their own tables and computers to complete the work. The local economy has recently fared poorly and Christina now has only enough work for herself. She made the best decision possible for her business by keeping to her budget and avoiding unnecessary cost burdens of an expensive lease. She has retained flexibility, greatly increasing her chances for very profitable results.

Planning Questions 6G

1. How long do you think your initial location and equipment provide adequate capacity for you to handle your business?

2. How will you handle your capacity situation if your operation gets very busy (will you add another shift, more equipment, more employees, more space)?

Evaluator's Thoughts

The initial capacity of the business gives the evaluator a feel for how much capacity you will require to manage your business effectively. Avoiding increases in space, equipment, and employees in times of temporary sales growth is a good way of preserving profit. However, if customer needs become compromised because the operations are strained and can no longer be handled sufficiently, expansion or some other alleviating alternative (more employees, equipment, subcontracting) is a must.

6H INFORMATION: How will you stay in touch with your operations?

Monitoring the operations area of your business can often lead to continual savings and improvement in customer service. One way of monitoring is to ask anyone involved. *Employees* performing daily tasks know the secrets to saving money and serving customers better and should be involved in formulating and improving the operations or delivery process. One way to find these secrets is to schedule regular meetings with employees or reward employees for suggestions. Trimming unnecessary costs and procedures is particularly important in a sluggish economy where sales revenues are down. You should eventually ask customers for their feedback to help you improve potential problem areas and reinforce any good things you have tried.

The method by which you stay abreast of feedback from your operations is technically known as a *management information system*. It should instead be called "knowing what's going on." The need to use up-to-date technology can be important in this regard since it can help with efficiency (computer systems in inventory and supplier management, for example) and error reduction, key elements in maintaining costs and improving operations to better serve customers. Technologically-related items could include computers, technical processes, customer service telephone lines or product testing devices as examples. A cost-effective and easy way to keep abreast of technology and its application to your business is to read magazines related to your type of industry.

Example

Matthew and Cocoa want to start Downtown Dining Restaurant and are considering the purchase of a computerized restaurant management system which would help in the operations, cost control, and service of the restaurant. When an order is entered into the system by waiting staff, the program signals areas of inventory that need replenishing. The system will also allow Downtown Dining to monitor its inventory levels ensuring that overstocking is not a problem. The manager simply issues a purchase order for the food and beverage items directly from the system and sends the order to a supplier. Since the system also keeps a record of all customer purchases, Matthew and Cocoa would be better able to plan menus according to their computer records of customer tastes.

Planning Questions 6H

1. What methods will you use to keep informed of your operations and improve them (employees, customers, comparison to competition)?

2. What information systems or technology are in place to help you ensure efficiency in your operations?

Evaluator's Thoughts

Here the evaluator is looking for ways in which you address the need to stay abreast of your operations and, ultimately, customer satisfaction. Since the operational area is the one most often ignored, addressing the elements covered in this chapter will clearly demonstrate your business insight. Show the evaluator that you have gone one step further by planning to stay on top of the ongoing operations.

6I ENVIRONMENT: What are your environmental implications?

The environmental movement has caused legislation to be enacted that protects the land, sea, and air from pollutants and waste. Some regions are more stringent than others. Businesses now review their operating practices to avoid legal problems or to be good corporate citizens. Ensure that any environmental implications of your type of business have been thought out, reviewed, and addressed. This could involve anything from hazardous materials that result from your operations to contaminated property under your building. Although you may not have caused the area to be contaminated, if you are the present owner you are probably legally responsible for cleaning it up. Check out any property purchases by requesting proof that it never was or is near a hazardous site. Your regional environment branch of the government can also assist you. If your business were to need financing in the future, it is important to note that financiers are becoming increasingly wary of getting involved with an environmentally haphazard company. The reason for this is that financiers could be legally responsible for cleaning up any environmental damage if forced to take over ownership of assets or property (pledged as collateral) in the event of default of loan payments. Outside of these legal ramifications, many companies have realized that cutting down on waste in various aspects of operations such as packaging, production, and transportation decreases costs and can be a strong selling point.

Example

When Victoria was considering starting Victoria's Perfume and Soap Company she was trying to think of ways to save money. She initially planned to offer the soaps and perfumes only in decorative bottles. However, she decided to reduce waste by making available large batches of perfume and bath oils in dispensers and allowing customers to bring their reused bottles back in for refill. This option for customers helped reduce her packaging costs, a savings she could pass on to her customers through lower prices. It also appealed to much of the target market of 25-45 year old females, many of whom are environmentally conscious.

Planning Questions 6I

1. Are there any environmental implications to your operations? If so, how does local legislation affect you?

2. Could you improve the cost of operations or increase customer appeal by considering environmental improvements that reduce waste?

Evaluator's Thoughts

The risk of causing environmental damage can lead to legal liability and health problems. This is not appealing to any investor, partner, bank, or employee. Therefore, carefully consider each aspect of your operation for possible environmental implications. If there are any, list the potential problem areas and how you will address them. Since an evaluator may not be completely familiar with your type of business, mentioning its environmental cleanliness will add one more positive to your business idea.

6J KEY SUCCESS FACTORS: How will you succeed?

Now that you have looked at your operations, you might start to see that certain issues are more important than others if you want to make your idea a success. Every business has certain *key success factors* that impact its ongoing success. These factors ensure that you can consistently offer your key features and competitive advantage. Some examples include keeping costs low, keeping a wide variety of stock on hand, having effective store managers, providing excellent customer service, or performing research to find new products. These are different than *basic product requirements* (Section 2B) because key success factors refer to the objective of your entire business and not just the essential requirements of one of your products or services. Knowing your key success factor(s) helps you understand your business and your market, giving you a key

Every firm has a key factor to its success.

objective to focus on both in starting up and as an ongoing business. If you become unsure at times of what areas to focus on to make your business a success, it will help to return to this section and remind yourself of these important factors. While there are many things a business must do well to be a success, each business will have only one or two *key* success factors rather than a lengthy list. Consider how you will achieve the stated success factor(s). Some common factors are listed in the side box.

EXAMPLES OF KEY SUCCESS FACTORS

- Inventory control
- Employee cost control
- Quality control
- Purchasing
- Manufacturing cost control
- Distribution
- Customer service
- Supplier relations
- Appealing product line
- Product quality
- Compensation policies
- Production scheduling
- Personnel training
- Supervision
- Manufacturing process
- Order processing efficiency

Example

Innovative Craft Imports Inc., a retail store, offers clients a wide array of artistic crafts imported from all over the world. The company has convenient hours, a pleasant helpful staff, a wide variety of stock, and reasonable prices as its features. Its competitive advantage is the innovative small crafts at reasonable prices. Customers can use these decoratives to provide a flair to their households. However, the overall key success factor is maintaining relationships with reliable suppliers who can provide the innovative imported crafts at reasonable prices. Without this the store would be unable to operate successfully.

Planning Questions 6J

1. What is/are your *key success factor(s)?* How can you ensure that this factor is maintained?

Evaluator's Thoughts

A key success factor is the vital element of your operations that will make your business successful. Identifying it and focusing on it will help you offer the key features and advantages that your customers desire.

6K COST OF OPERATIONS: How much will it cost to run your business?

Once you have considered various aspects of your operations, you can begin to attach costs to the options. Some of the key costs can be summarized in this section and will become the basis of your initial profit projections in Chapter 8 **FINANCIAL**. For now, try to determine only approximate costs that you think you would incur starting and running your business. If you cannot think of certain ones, do them later. As you continue to think and find real costs, you can revise the numbers. Your costs can be broken down into *fixed expenses* (costs that stay relatively the same month-to-month regardless of the amount of your sales) such as rent or utilities. The other type of costs are known as *variable expenses*. These are costs related to each order sold such as delivery cost, ingredients, packaging, and so on that vary directly with the number of orders you have (unlike fixed expenses). Expenses vary according to the type of business. There could be initial one-time expenses such as renovations to install an office in your home, ongoing fixed expenses such as equipment maintenance (as with a photography studio or landscaping business), or other items specific to your situation that were not directly covered in this chapter.

The Idea Guide

Planning Questions 6K

NOTE: The spaces provided are to help you get started. You may need more space as you consider all of the costs associated with your idea.

1. For your location (6A question 1), how much would it cost you per month (this will be a *fixed expense* since the amount to be paid stays the same every month)? Are there any other fixed expenses associated with this location (such as utilities or maintenance fees)?

LOCATION EXPENSES

LOCATION	COST PER MONTH	FIXED OR VARIABLE?

2. In 6B you identified key services or products required from suppliers that you will sell or use to make your product (such as the cost of mail order articles in the Hugh and Maria example in 6E). These services and items related to your product or service are *variable* expenses. List them below.

SUPPLY EXPENSES

KEY ITEMS/SERVICES FROM SUPPLIERS REQUIRED IN EACH PRODUCT YOU SELL	COST PER ITEM	# ITEMS REQUIRED IN EACH PRODUCT	TOTAL COST OF ITEM per PRODUCT SOLD

3. Refer to 6C and identify the costs involved in taking an order and processing it (credit card commission, phone charge, commission, credit check cost, postage, delivery, handling, etc.). These would be *variable* expenses. An example would be a credit card charge of 2% per transaction.

ORDER PROCESSING EXPENSES

NATURE OF COST	COST per ITEM

4. Refer to Section 6D and identify approximate costs incurred if you are required to pay for handling of items as part of delivering your service or product (duties, taxes, gas for truck). These are *variable* expenses since they vary with how many products you sell or contracts you acquire.

HANDLING AND DELIVERY EXPENSES

ITEM	COST per ITEM

5. In 6E, the importance of maintaining efficient levels of inventory was discussed. If you require inventory to sell to your customers or inventory of necessary parts to help you provide service to them, what will be your average inventory requirement? Use the following table to determine amounts. Once you receive an order, the original cost of the item to you (shown by the *approximate cost per unit* in table) will become a variable expense since it is an expense associated with the sale of an item.

INVENTORY COSTS

ITEMS	APPROXIMATE NUMBER OF UNITS	APPROXIMATE COST per UNIT	TOTAL

6. Refer to 6F and identify the approximate cost of each of your equipment requirements. When are they needed?

EQUIPMENT REQUIREMENTS

EQUIPMENT	COST	WHEN (now or future)

7. In 6H the importance of keeping informed of your operations is discussed. What are the costs for anything required to help you stay in touch with the performance of your operations (computers, computer programs, customer toll-free lines, etc.)?

INFORMATION REQUIREMENTS

ITEM	COST	WHEN (now or future)

8. In 6I the environmental implications of operations were discussed. What would be the costs for you to comply with legislation? Is this a fixed expense (initial licensing fee, for example) or variable expense (an incurred cost per each item sold)?

ENVIRONMENTAL EXPENSES

ITEM	COST	FIXED OR VARIABLE

9. Refer to 6K and identify other specific expenditures required initially or on an ongoing basis (such as legal fees, signs, phone lines, business cards, cleaning supplies)?

OTHER EXPENDITURES

NATURE OF COST	AMOUNT	WHEN (INITIALLY OR ONGOING)

Evaluator's Thoughts

This section helps you sort out the operational costs of your idea. Breaking out your costs also assists an evaluator in understanding the cost implications of your type of business. Evaluators keep financial implications of all aspects of your business in the back of their mind as they read your plan. If you want to make sure that the strengths of your business idea come through, try and make your proposal user-friendly. Tables like those in this section help sort out your costs (initially for your own benefit and later for an evaluator). Evaluators, like everyone else, prefer things presented as simply as possible.

7 PERSONNEL:

Hiring and Managing Employees

Chapters 1-4 of this guide discussed in order: the importance of knowing yourself, your idea, your market, and your competition when planning a business. You then used this foundation in Chapter 5 to begin to think of possible plans to market your idea and, in Chapter 6, an operational design that would support it. This chapter discusses the people that will make all of this happen. It is important to consider your personnel requirements and the type of people who will fill them.

Here is something you probably already know, but as a business owner you will need to continually remind yourself of it. Business owners who surround themselves with talented individuals and encourage their input and ideas, rather than merely hiring non-threatening people to simply execute the owner's orders, will always be the most successful.

7A MANAGEMENT TEAM

Identify areas of your business idea requiring close attention.

7B OPERATIONS PERSONNEL

Consider your hiring requirements and ways to attract motivated, effective employees.

7C ADVISORS

Consider the availability of outside individuals who can provide you with advice.

7D PERSONNEL DEVELOPMENT

Identify areas of your business that may require future employees, development, or training.

7E COMPENSATION

Consider possible ways to attract talented employees and individuals.

7A MANAGEMENT TEAM: Who will manage your business?

Most business owners try to juggle many different roles in the beginning. However, some are able and willing to hire help to manage areas of their business. This section will help you consider any required management positions and the skills needed to perform it well. This will help you identify an individual who could potentially handle the position. The person preferably has relevant experience, in addition to appropriate training and accomplishments. A well-rounded management team with business skills across marketing, accounting, and operations is the ideal situation, but not always realistic for a small business. Instead the *operations* area is usually the priority. For example, a construction company needs experienced on-site foremen while a retail store may require an experienced retail manager but both could do without a marketing manager (Section 7C **Key Advisors** helps you address situations where you cannot afford to staff every key function). Another way of strengthening your management area is by having a *succession plan*. Succession plans refer to the development of future management talent should, for any reason, the present managers be forced to vacate. These could, for example, be assistant managers or other employees who could be promoted should a key manager leave. Having a succession plan ensures that the continuity of your business is well insured.

Managers for your company usually become well-trained in how your business is carried on and are often exposed to sensitive information on pricing, marketing, or financial performance. To reduce the possibility that an employee or manager may use this information to start up a competing venture, business owners sometimes negotiate a *non-competitive agreement* at the time the person is hired. This is a legal agreement in which the employee agrees to refrain from starting a competing business, and is a necessity for firms dealing with research or innovative technologies.

Example

Derek was starting a business, Food Presenters, to distribute food products for small food manufacturers. He wrote the following description about a marketing manager position that he was filling:

"Marketing Manager This responsibility will involve creating an overall marketing plan to achieve access to the target market of supermarket chains. This position will also assist in selling the benefits of using Food Presenters as a supermarket distribution company to small food manufacturerst".

Food Presenters has hired Donna who has 5 years in consumer products marketing with a large food manufacturer. Time spent in both sales and product management gives her an appreciation for the grocery business clientele. She has experience in negotiating with the grocery trade as both a sales representative and marketing manager. This will allow her to create effective marketing plans while setting realistic marketing and sales objectives.

Planning Questions 7A

1. Will you need managers initially? If so, describe the position required, its responsibilities, and any individuals (along with their related skills, qualifications, or experience) whom you have identified as possible managers. If you will not require managers, explain why.

MANAGEMENT REQUIREMENTS

POSITION	RESPONSIBILITIES	NAME AND QUALIFICATIONS

2. Do you have the resume of each individual? Does your type of product necessitate the signing of non-competitive agreements by your managers in case they decide to leave and start a similar venture?

Evaluator's Thoughts

The evaluator tries to ascertain whether a business has at least some managers with knowledge of the type of business in question. Whether the management skills complement each other is also an indicator of how a company will handle decision-making on key issues. Succession plans for managers are a good indicator of future continuity of business performance. If the business has one manager (like many startups), the evaluator considers whether the duties of the business are too diverse to be handled by one individual. If you are a sole owner/manager, show that you are able to handle the important functions that relate to the operations of the business, since issues like marketing are less important than the initial operational performance of the business. If your skill is marketing, then show how the operations are either being handled by someone else or are very simple.

7B OPERATIONS PERSONNEL: Will you require help?

In Chapter 6, you considered the operations aspect of your business. This section refers to the "people part" of those operations, a key matter to consider. High quality work generally requires skilled employees. If none are available, you could face high training costs and operational difficulties until the trainees are up to speed. This can affect your performance and financial success. Some new businesses get by without hiring anyone. One way is to *subcontract* required jobs to other businesses or skilled individuals who can help on an as-needed basis. This allows you to avoid keeping very high wage-earning people on your payroll when you first start out or minimize any training costs involved. If you do need to hire, your wage level should generally reflect the *level of skill* required

> **A business is no more than a collection of individuals' talents.**

of your employees. However, there are other factors in finding, keeping, and motivating employees. Business owners that treat employees as commodities will face high turnover, absenteeism, and poor morale; these effects can threaten the success of the business and add to the risk of the entire venture. On the other hand, a business that treats its employees with respect will fulfill one of the key requirements for business success.

Some businesses have observed that having an individual performing one task repetitively can cause boredom and motivation problems resulting in errors. Therefore, personnel is rotated to perform different tasks, or they are given an entire assignment to do rather than continually completing one small portion. Studies have shown that this can improve morale, reduce errors, and improve quality since a person is motivated by the increased accountability of performing the entire job. Another way to address an employee's accountability is to provide formal feedback periodically through the year. In addition to informal daily feedback, a formal report can help an employee by discussing their progress, strengths, and areas that could be improved upon. Use your own and your friends' experiences as employees when thinking about arranging a motivated, content, and efficient workforce. Note the factors that will prevent a union from establishing and making excessive demands on the business operations. Again, these factors are likely related to how well you treat your employees. If you are required to hire union employees, study the legislation that requires it and the conditions you must meet.

Example

Ricardo started a consulting firm to help small businesses become more efficient through the use of computerized administrative functions. He is an excellent computer systems designer and very personable. Therefore, he would concentrate on consulting and marketing. However, Ricardo knew he would require very skilled individuals who could program and implement his design for the customer so that he could go on to the next project. Rather than hiring employees, he decided to subcontract the programming out to freelance computer programmers who would work for him on an as-needed basis. Since his small business clients could not afford to pay excessively, Ricardo was able to keep his prices down by hiring skilled independent individuals who would not require the expensive payroll benefits of normal employees. His clients did not even know or care that these individuals were not his employees since their job was completed as promised for a very good price.

Planning Question 7B

1. Referring to Chapter 6 **BUSINESS OPERATIONS**, for which aspect(s) of your operations will you initially require personnel (such as a receptionist or store manager, for example)? Do you have any hiring criteria in mind regarding required education level, training, experience, ability, and so on?

PERSONNEL REQUIREMENTS

TYPE OF POSITION	HIRING CRITERIA

Evaluator's Thoughts

The evaluator looks to see that the business owner has considered a hiring criteria to acquire competent staff, and policies to keep them content. Overall, the evaluator wants to see that the business owner is surrounded by competent employees who can deliver the promised benefits to customers.

7C ADVISORS: Will you have outside help?

Advisors are individuals or friends who are not involved in your day-to-day operations but can be relied upon for advice and insight into matters such as marketing, business planning, financial matters, and personnel. Access to advisors offers you a broad base of available knowledge and expertise to provide input to your company direction. Advisors can also be

Key advisors can help legitimize a small business to evaluators.

LOW-COST EXPERTISE

- Available professionals
- Employees in related business
- Volunteer board of directors

employees or managers related to your specific industry such as experienced people in construction, retail, technology, etc. Another option could be setting up a volunteer board of directors of experienced business people (from large or small companies) who can meet with you every few months to review objectives and performance. You will probably find that most people are flattered if approached to assist in advising a business venture.

Example

*Patricia started Permanently Temporary (original example in Section 5B **Marketing Mix**) to provide temporary personnel for local businesses. She has asked her friend Jane, an experienced accountant with a local firm, to act as an advisor. Jane's extensive experience with small businesses allows*

Patricia to consult an experienced advisor on financial and strategy issues. She has also asked Anita, who is a colleague of a friend, to advise her. Anita is a personnel manager in another city, and will assist her with quarterly planning. Anita can provide insight on how Permanently Temporary's marketing can best be tailored to persuade personnel managers.

Planning Question 7C

1. Are you potentially lacking in a key area of management or knowledge about your type of business? If so, identify any advisors you could possibly find and their area of specialty.

KEY ADVISORS

AREA REQUIRING HELP	NAME OF ADVISOR	QUALIFICATIONS

2. Do you think you could convince any experienced local business people to act as an informal board of directors to give you feedback on your business direction? If so, outline who they would be.

Evaluator's Thoughts

A business is as good as its management. Therefore, evaluators analyze management to detect areas that a business has left uncovered. Businesses that show initiative by recruiting individuals to cover these areas demonstrate that they have access to talented individuals to help with important ongoing management issues. This influences an evaluator to believe more strongly in the business. Try to show at least one or two advisors in key areas (if they are friends you don't have to mention it). Attracting the voluntary help of talented individuals reinforces the promise of your business idea.

7D PERSONNEL DEVELOPMENT: What will you need in the future?

If you are not able to hire for all of the positions you require immediately, this section allows you to think about the management or staff area that needs to be developed in the future (such as a customer service representative, skilled employee, or marketing manager) to ensure that the business remains competitive. Perhaps you need certain skills developed in your employees to keep up with change to your type of business or to ensure that you remain competitive   Staff training ensures that the functions they are performing on your behalf are completed effectively. This will help your business grow profitably and allow the business to maintain a positive image among your many audiences such as suppliers, customers, peer companies with which you network, lenders, and employees. All forward-thinking companies remain competitive because they recognize the value of a staff that is competent and well-trained.

POSSIBLE STAFF TRAINING

- computer software training
- relevant technical courses
- sales training
- marketing courses
- telephone training
- negotiating skills
- customer service training

Planning Questions 7D

1. What are the key staff positions that could be added in the future? When?

FUTURE PERSONNEL REQUIREMENTS

FUTURE STAFF POSITIONS	WHEN REQUIRED

2. What key skills may have to be developed in the future? How are you dealing with any shortage of skills that may exist in the beginning?

Evaluator's Thoughts

When a business takes the initiative to address future developmental areas, an evaluator cannot help but be impressed. It shows an understanding of how to remain successful.

7E COMPENSATION: How much will you pay your staff?

You may be able to find the best employees, but can you afford the salary? As mentioned in Section 6K **Cost of Operations**, an important consideration for small businesses is to avoid potential cash drains through excessive *fixed costs* (costs such as salaries that must be paid regardless of how many sales are made). These fixed salaries to you or your staff can become a burden in periods of slower sales, especially a startup situation. In addition, how you compensate yourself can have tax implications. Before deciding on your compensation, consider what form of ownership (sole proprietorship, partnership, or corporation) you will likely use. This is discussed in the Appendix D **Legal Considerations**. If your business is particularly complicated, an accountant can guide you. The issue of compensating employees is another issue. If you are certain that a salary is necessary to attract a motivated individual *and* you can afford it, then perhaps this is a good route for you. In new or growing companies, you may be able to attract competent managers or key employees by augmenting salary with a small percentage of the profits and/or ownership or bonuses based on company achievement (*variable expenses* since they are only paid bonuses if sales levels warrant). This can reduce your fixed costs and motivate a management staff or key employees by providing incentive to achieve.

ADVANTAGES FOR SMALL FIRM EMPLOYEES

- Creativity
- Responsibility
- More input
- Less rigid structure
- Participate in growth
- Profit sharing

The downside is that you give up a portion of ownership or profits of the business. However, an incentive arrangement may help your business to attain more profit than you would have made with a standard salary arrangement. If giving up some control of ownership concerns you, an agreement with staff whereby you retain full authority can be arranged. A lawyer can best advise you.

It should be noted that not all managers or key employees are attracted to a small business because of money or ownership. Some would prefer to work in a small business environment after having worked in the depths of a larger corporation. They enjoy the added responsibility, challenge, and accountability and would welcome the opportunity despite less pay. Others will work initially for little pay to participate in what they see as inevitable long-term growth which will help propel them to a senior position in a growing company. One option is to pay people as a consultant, rather than as an employee, which saves you and them tax since you do not have to pay payroll benefits and they can write off many of their expenses such as car and home office. In this case, you can probably pay them less than they would make working for anyone else and they still come out ahead with the write-offs. An accountant can help you decide which way is best. Whichever way you do decide to proceed, try to reflect on your experience as an employee as it may tell you everything you need to know. As anyone who has worked on a successful project or in a successful business knows, the right motivated people around you can help propel you to heights you never would have achieved alone. This principle refers to all levels of your business from managers to operations employees.

Motivated employees help businesses achieve success.

Example

Matthew and Cocoa decided to start the Downtown Dining Restaurant and hired Helen, previously a manager with one of the most successful establishments in their area. Helen is known for her innovative marketing programs that successfully attract a large corporate clientele for banquets and meetings. Helen would normally command a very high salary but was attracted by an offer of 10% ownership of the new restaurant. Helen was impressed by Downtown Dining's plans, seeing good potential for its growth in the local market. Matthew and Cocoa know that Helen will be motivated by her ownership participation which can only help them.

Planning Questions 7E

1. What are you paying yourself and your key managers (salary amount, bonuses, etc.)? How will you attract any necessary key employees or managers?

2. In Section 7B you identified the type of employees your operation would require. How much would you pay these people per year/job/hour? Identify if the employees are paid a salary or wage (both *fixed costs* since a salary or wage per person does not change with the amount produced) or by the job or unit sold (both *variable* expenses since the amount you pay will vary according to how many jobs or units you sell).

Evaluator's Thoughts

Salaries in general, whether to an owner or manager, can be a large cash burden. Excessive compensation can seriously inhibit the ability of a business to deal with unforeseen future financial matters. Show how you are able to attract quality individuals, compensate them, and have them contribute to your future profitability.

CONCLUSION: PART 2

Results of Steps 5, 6, and 7

In the second section of the guide (Chapters 5,6, and 7), you covered ways to communicate the benefits of using your product to the target market of potential buyers. Next, you began to consider what you would need to put in place in order to produce the product or service, get it to a customer, and manage it on an ongoing basis. Finally, you identified areas that would require additional people to assist you in running the operation effectively, both in the beginning and into the future.

Great work! You have gotten farther than 99% of all people who have business ideas. Many of these individuals who have done less preparation than you have actually started a business. However, starting a business is easy. Making it a success is the challenge. As mentioned in the foreword of the guide, people who dive in without preparation make up the majority of business failures.

You have met the major part of the challenge by the preparation that you have done in these pages. Even though you have done a great deal more than most people, the next section is highly recommended. It will further refine your idea by helping you set some goals and objectives. Why is this important? Consider the future for a moment. You are ready to put your idea into place or you have already started. Some of the following events could occur:

- You need a loan from a bank or relative to start or expand the business
- You want to find a partner
- You want to ensure that you are paying the correct amount of taxes
- You are considering opening a new location managed by another person
- Selling the idea to others has entered your mind

In each of these scenarios, the various affected parties will require not only the information that you have provided in the first sections of the guide but additional information to clarify the expected sales and expenses involved, the amount of money required, and the future objectives of the business. The next three chapters allow you to do this.

Just as budgeting for household expenditures, renovations, or personal finances can help you consider and clarify your objectives (and eliminate possibly expensive, unnecessary steps), setting some simple financial objectives can keep you on the right track. Doing it for yourself at the very outset can help you understand your idea even more thoroughly and is a crucial step to business success. In several steps you have already entered approximate cost estimates of various aspects of the business. The financial section ahead merely takes these numbers and summarizes them in a standard business format ideal for relating the potential of the idea to others.

8 FINANCIAL:

Details of the Money Involved

NOTE: This chapter contains simple principles and examples on determining the profitability and viability of your venture. It is meant for demonstrative purposes and should not replace the advice of a professional accountant.

After analyzing the many factors that can affect your idea such as the characteristics of the market and the competition, you have outlined some preliminary plans for marketing your idea and the requirements to make your operations effective. This section allows you to make some financial projections using all of this information you have already covered. Considering the financial potential is a key step in preparing an idea. There are several reasons why people want to start their own business. These include wanting a challenge, feeling independent, not having to answer to a boss, or simply feeling good about doing something they like to do. However, the one thing that everybody has in common is curiosity of the financial implications of starting up and maintaining their own business. This section allows you to address this. Even if you will have someone else prepare your business finances, reading this chapter will provide you with a clear understanding of what exactly the person is preparing for you. As mentioned, the chapter simply uses the information you have previously considered and demonstrates how to project your financial results.

8A INCOME STATEMENT

Compile your expected revenues and expenses to determine a projected profit.

8B CASH FLOW STATEMENT

Consider the cash implications of your projections.

8C BREAK-EVEN POINT

Determine how many orders you must sell to break-even.

8D FINANCIAL RECORDS

Consider the implications of maintaining regular financial information.

8E ASSUMPTIONS

List the realistic assumptions that were used in your financial projections.

8F FINANCIAL REQUIREMENTS

Determine what amount of money you would require to start.

8A INCOME STATEMENT: How much profit will you make?

To determine just how much money you could make with your idea, it is helpful to consider the adage "you have to spend money to make money". In Section 5E **Pricing** and Section 6K **Cost of Operations**, the issues of expenditures of money were briefly introduced. Operating expenses are incurred in the normal course of doing business (see list of various expenses below). Certain expenses incurred are directly related to the sale of each unit of your product or service. These are known as *variable expenses* since their total *varies* depending on how many units you sell or produce. These expenses include items such as commissions to sales staff, delivery charges, handling costs, ingredients costs, and so on. All other expenses are related to your administration, marketing, or operations and can be classified as *fixed expenses* since they are predictable and stay relatively the same (or "fixed") regardless of your sales level. These are costs such as rent, wages, maintenance, and other expenses not directly related to the product or service itself.

VARIOUS OPERATING EXPENSES	
• Salary	• Telephone
• Wages	• Accounting
• Promotion	• Selling
• Maintenance	• Supplies
• Rent	• Bank charges
• Distribution	• Utilities
• Loan interest	• Legal

When all of your expenses are subtracted from your total revenues (sales), you will arrive at an income or *profit* figure. An *income statement* (sometimes called a *profit and loss statement*) is simply a record of your total revenue and total expenses over a monthly or yearly period. A *projected* income statement is a forecast of your *expected* revenue and expenses over a *future* monthly or yearly period. Most small, large, and new businesses prepare a projected income statement to plan for the forthcoming year. Since sales and expenses can fluctuate monthly in seasonal businesses (Section 3D **Special Considerations**) or startup situations, it is important for a small business to project its revenues and expenses at the beginning of each year on a *monthly* basis. Sales projections should also be realistic and conservative to allow you to truly determine whether you can cover your operating expenses. "Projections" are rarely 100% accurate but give you an idea of the costs and profit you can expect. Sales and costs projections can be revised as the year progresses, based on your actual results to date.

You determine your *total sales* by multiplying your expected number of units to be sold during a particular month by the price that you will charge. If you recall, in Section 5F **Sales Objective** various factors were considered in determining what your sales per month and per year would be.

Example

The following example shows the 5 steps in preparing a projected income statement. The resulting statement for TJ's Specialty Coffee Shop is shown on page 76.

1. Determine your estimated *number of sales orders* (*or units*) *per month*. Each month can be different. Multiply this by your *price* to arrive at your *total sales revenue* for the month.

Tom and Jennifer estimated that their sales for TJ's Specialty Coffee Shop would be about $47,000 (refer back to the example in Section 5F). However, after further consideration, they believed that coffee sales would fluctuate by season. They estimated that they would have 80 orders each day at $2.00 per order for a total of $4800 sales orders for each fall and winter month (80 x $2.00 x 30 days). For each spring and summer month, they estimated sales of 50 orders per day at $2.00 for a monthly total of $3000 (50 x $2.00 x 30 days).

2. Calculate all of the variable expenses associated with each sale of a product or service. This becomes your *cost of sale* for each order. Multiplying this cost of sale figure by the number of sales orders (not sales revenue) in step 1 above gives you your *total* cost of sales for each month.

Their variable expenses associated with each $2.00 order were: coffee beans (15 cents), cup (5 cents), lid on cup (3 cents), cream (3 cents), sugar (4 cents), and muffin (which they had *supplied for 30 cents each from a local bakery). Adding up the costs revealed a cost of sale of 60 cents per order. The total cost of sales per month in the busy fall and winter season would be approximately $1440 per month (60 cent cost of each order multiplied by the expected 2400 monthly orders). The total monthly cost of sales in the quiet spring and summer season would be approximately $900 (60 cents x 1500 monthly orders).*

3. Subtract the monthly cost of sales in step 2 from your total monthly revenue figures in step 1. The resulting number is your *monthly gross profit (also called gross margin).*

Therefore, TJ's projected gross profit would be approximately $3360 in each of the busy months ($4800 sales less $1440 cost of goods sold). The gross profit in the quiet months was projected at approximately $2100 ($3000 sales less $900 cost of goods sold).

4. Calculate the monthly *total operating expenses* (monthly fixed expenses such as rent, utilities, maintenance, and advertising, of which many were determined in 6K **Cost of Operations** and 5D **Marketing Budget**) associated with your monthly operations and when they occur (some may occur only in certain months).

Tom and Jennifer figured their other operating expenses (fixed expenses) to include rent ($500 per month), utilities ($50 per month), and insurance ($50 per month). Also, a cashier was required in the busy winter months at $10 per hour for 30 hours a week (which is 120 hours per month for a total $1200 per month) and 15 hours in the quiet warmer months (for a monthly total of 60 hours or $600 per month). Other monthly expenses included advertising ($300 per month during the busy season and $100 in the quiet ones), and maintenance (budgeted at $300 per month in the busy season and $150 the rest of the year). When summed these become their projected monthly operating expenses (see projected statement page 76).

5. Subtracting the total of your monthly operating expenses from the gross profit (see step 3 above) gives you a monthly net profit before taxes. Adding the columns left to right gives yearly totals.

They then subtracted all of the above expenses from their sales total to arrive at their projected net profit before taxes figure. See the example projected income statement on the next page. Note that the calculated figures related to steps 1 to 5 are indicated by the appropriate step number in the far left-hand column on TJ's projected income statement.

In the TJ's Specialty Coffee Shop example, it is likely that Tom and Jennifer would require equipment such as a coffee maker and dishwasher. You may have noticed that the purchase of these items does not appear on the income statement. When preparing an income statement, *cost of purchases* of equipment, vehicles, or real estate (all are referred to as *capital purchases*) are *not included* as an operating expense. Why? Because the item purchased likely has a useful performance life of several years (and not just the one year in which it was purchased) and so the cost is allocated over this useful period of the asset. This process is known as calculating the *depreciation* of the asset. In addition, any expenses associated with using equipment or property (maintenance, interest, fuel, depreciation) in the course of your business must also be included as an ongoing expense of running your business.

Example

TJ's purchased coffee making equipment costing $3600 in Year 1. They believed the equipment would need replacing in 4 years. Therefore, they divided $3600 by 4 to get a yearly depreciation of $900. Since they were preparing a monthly income statement, they divided the $900 yearly figure by 12 months to arrive at $75 per month in depreciation expense. Note that the depreciation of $75 has been included in the projected monthly statement on the next page.

The Idea Guide

To summarize, the *original purchase price* of the business asset is allocated over the *expected life* of the asset, and this allocated portion (along with the expenses in maintaining the asset) are considered expenses on your income statement. The expected useful life of various classes of assets (such as computers, buildings, or equipment) are different and correspondingly the depreciation will differ among various assets that you purchase. Your local tax revenue department or accountant can give you the applicable depreciation schedule to apply in your local tax jurisdiction. The benefit to businesses of including depreciation expense is that it lowers their profit figure, meaning less tax to be paid.

TJ's SPECIALTY COFFEE SHOP PROJECTED INCOME STATEMENT: (January-December Year 1)

Steps*		Jan	Feb	Mar	Apr	May	Jun	July	Aug	Sept	Oct	Nov	Dec	TOTAL
	REVENUE													
1	Sales	4800	4800	4800	4800	3000	3000	3000	3000	3000	3000	4800	4800	46800
2	Cost of sales	1440	1440	1440	1440	900	900	900	900	900	900	1440	1440	14040
3	**Gross Profit**	**3360**	**3360**	**3360**	**3360**	**2100**	**2100**	**2100**	**2100**	**2100**	**2100**	**3360**	**3360**	**32760**
	OPERATING EXPENSES													
	Wages	1200	1200	1200	1200	600	600	600	600	600	600	1200	1200	10800
	Advertising	300	300	300	300	100	100	100	100	100	100	300	300	2400
	Maintenance	300	300	300	300	150	150	150	150	150	150	300	300	2700
	Rent	500	500	500	500	500	500	500	500	500	500	500	500	6000
	Utilities	50	50	50	50	50	50	50	50	50	50	50	50	600
	Insurance	50	50	50	50	50	50	50	50	50	50	50	50	600
	Depreciation	75	75	75	75	75	75	75	75	75	75	75	75	900
4	**Total Operating Expenses**	**2475**	**2475**	**2475**	**2475**	**1525**	**1525**	**1525**	**1525**	**1525**	**1525**	**2475**	**2475**	**24000**
5	**Net Profit Before Tax**	**885**	**885**	**885**	**885**	**575**	**575**	**575**	**575**	**575**	**575**	**885**	**885**	**8760**

*This column of numbers relates to the 5 steps to constructing an income statement used in the example.

Example

NOTE: The next example uses the same 5 steps as the previous example. The resulting projected income statement for the first 4 months appears on page 81. (The full 12 months is in Appendix E).

*1. Lightcost Lighting (original example in Section 5E **Pricing**) determined its initial monthly sales to be one sale of a lighting system installation every month based on its initial assumptions of installing entire floors of lighting at a time. The owner, Philip, estimated that by Month 3 he would be completing 3 to 4 installation projects. He also thought that he would likely increase this even more as the year progressed but wanted to be conservative in his estimates. His sale revenue was estimated at an average $2500 per floor of a project so 3 floors completed per month would be $7500 revenue per month and 4 floors $10,000 per month.*

2. The variable costs associated with each floor of a project would be the cost of lighting supplies and components ($300) and fees paid to an installation company ($700 per floor) for a total of $1000 cost of sale per floor of installed lighting. Therefore, when he estimated 3 floors of installation in Month 3, a total of $3000 cost of sales would occur for the month.

3. Lightcost Lighting's gross profit on each project would be approximately $1500 per floor (based on $2500 sales revenue less $1000 cost of sales) or 60% of the selling price.

4. The other operating expenses include rent at $300 per month, insurance ($100), and interest ($125) on his long-term truck loan. His other fixed operating expenses were related to advertising (between $200-$400 per month), telephone (between $50-75), and depreciation on his truck of $375 per month ($18,000 purchase price divided over a useful life of 4 years or 48 months).

5. Philip subtracted all of the above operating expenses to arrive at a monthly net profit before tax figure. The resulting full year projected income statement appears in Appendix E. An abbreviated four-month version of the projected income statement appears on page 81.

Planning Questions 8A

NOTE: These 5 questions use the same 5 steps as the previous examples. An income statement worksheet has been provided on the next page to which you can transfer the following answers.

1. Using the information from Section 5F (**Sales Objectives**), estimate an *Amount of Sales Orders* for each month (if you have more than one product, make other charts like the one below). Remember: seasonality or other factors may affect sales levels in certain months. Using your *Price* on line B below (set in Section 5E **Pricing**), what would be the total *Sales Revenue* (line C) for each month?

MONTH	1	2	3	4	5	6	7	8	9	10	11	12
A) # of Sales Orders												
B) Price per Order												
C) Monthly Sales Revenue (A x B)												

2. Calculate all of the variable expenses (commissions, ingredients, components, cost of item) associated with each sale of your product or service. Many were identified as *variable expenses* in Chapter 6 (Section 6K **Cost of Operations** questions 2, 3, 4, 5 and Section 5E **Pricing** question 4). Add up these variable expenses to arrive at a *Total Cost of Sale* for each unit. If you have employees paid by the *job* or *order,* it would be included here also (refer to Section 7E **Compensation** question 2). Multiply the *Total Cost of Sale* by the *Quantity of Orders* for each month in question 1 to determine your monthly *Cost of Sales*. Make a separate chart for each product or service that you will offer.

VARIABLE EXPENSES ASSOCIATED WITH EACH SALE

TYPE OF VARIABLE EXPENSE	COST(add this column to get Total Cost of Sale)
TOTAL COST OF SALE	

MONTH	1	2	3	4	5	6	7	8	9	10	11	12
# of Sales Orders												
Cost of Sales												

3. Subtract the monthly *Cost of Sales* in question 2 from your total *Monthly Sales Revenue* figure from question 1. This result becomes your *Monthly Gross Profit.*

MONTH	1	2	3	4	5	6	7	8	9	10	11	12
Monthly Gross Profit (=Sales-Cost of Sales)												

The Idea Guide

NOTE: The figures Monthly Sales Revenue (question 1), Monthly Cost of Sales (question 2) and Monthly Gross Profit (question 3) can be transferred to the Income Statement Worksheet provided below. Questions 4 and 5 can be answered directly on the worksheet.

4. Estimate all other operating expenses associated with your monthly operations. Some months will be different than others. These were recorded in Sections 2C **Legal Issues** question 2, Section 5D **Marketing Budget** question 1, Section 6K **Cost of Operations** (questions 1, 7, 8, and 9), and Section 7E **Compensation** (questions 1 and 2).

5. Subtracting all of your operating expenses from your gross profit gives you your net profit before taxes. Adding up the columns left to right gives you your *projected* totals for the year. Include an approximate tax rate (available from the revenue department) to determine your *Net Profit after Tax.*

MONTHLY INCOME STATEMENT WORKSHEET

		MONTH												
		1	2	3	4	5	6	7	8	9	10	11	12	Total
	REVENUE													
1	**Sales**													
2	**Cost of sales**													
3	**Gross Profit** *(step 1-step 2)*													
	OPERATING EXPENSES													
4	**Total Operating Expenses**													
5	**Net Profit Before Tax** *(step 3-step 4)*													
	Estimated Tax(Rate__%)													
	Net Profit After Tax													

Note: The digits 1 to 5 in the left hand column are the same 5 steps used to construct the examples in Section 8A

8B CASH FLOW STATEMENT: When will you receive cash from sales?

An *income statement* details sales and related expenses. A *cash flow statement* shows the details of actual cash flowing into and out of the business and the running total of cash. It is derived from the income statement. A cash flow statement includes *outflows* such as the purchase of materials, office supplies, loan repayments, and cash *inflows* such as cash collected from sales. Because it monitors all cash inflows and outflows, a cash flow statement signals any ongoing cash surpluses or deficits that might arise and essentially predicts what will happen in your bank account. It will also assist you in determining the initial cash requirements of a business.

Although a cash flow statement appears to be the same as an income statement, the difference between the two can be seen more clearly by use of the Lightcost Lighting example shown on page 81. When sales for a month total $2500 in Month 1, this number is listed as the sales revenue for month 1

CASH FLOW CONSIDERATIONS

- Seasonal sales
- Credit sales
- Project-based work
- Credit granted by a supplier
- High levels of inventory

in the income statement. However, the entire $2500 might *not* be received in Month 1 since some customers buy on credit and actually pay sometime in the future. Therefore, the $2500 figure in the income statement does not give us an accurate picture of when the cash from sales are collected. Why is this important? It is important because a business can be profitable and have what is known as *cash flow problems* (first mentioned in Section 6C **Order Processing**).

A cash flow problem occurs when a company runs short of cash and has difficulty carrying on its daily operations (paying employees, suppliers, or landlords). A cash flow statement is a key management tool for most businesses, particularly those businesses with the characteristics of credit sales (accounts receivable) or project-based work where costs are incurred long before revenues are received. Examples of businesses in which cash flow analysis is particularly important are listed in the box above.

Example

*Philip noticed that his Lightcost Lighting projected income statement (section 8A **Income Statement**) indicated that his lighting projects would be very profitable. However, he found out through discussions with building managers that he would be paid for his work approximately 30-60 days after his project was completed. Philip had anticipated collecting his invoiced amount from all customers 30 days after the project completed. However, the managers of large buildings said that their companies would take extra time, some even up to 90 days. Philip was concerned as he had to pay suppliers for lighting materials immediately upon receipt and had to pay the installation company upon completion of a project. He constructed a projected cash flow statement (the abbreviated 4-month portion of his projected cash flow appears on page 81 and full year in Appendix E) using the following assumptions:*

- *Lightcost Lighting's sales projections were determined in the previous example and are shown on both Line 1 in the income statement and Line B in the cash flow statement)*

- *After his conversations with building managers, Philip estimated that 30% of his building customers would pay his invoice after 30 days, 50% after 60 days, and 20% after 90 days. None would pay cash immediately upon a sale or in less than 30 days. (Lines D, E and F)*

- *The installation company (Philip did not have his own employees) and suppliers of lighting materials had to be paid immediately after completion of an installation. (Lines N and O)*

- *The operating expenses on his income statement (interest, rent, insurance, advertising, telephone) had to be paid in the month that they were incurred. (Lines M, P, Q, R, and S)*

- *He would buy the truck for $18,000 from a dealer. Since the original purchase of the truck involved an actual cash outflow from his bank account, he would include the initial truck purchase as a one-time outflow (Line K, Month 1).*

- *He would finance the truck purchase with a loan from the bank and the loan proceeds as a one-time inflow (on Line H, Month 1) on his cash flow statement. It would not be included on his projected income statement since it was not revenue from business operations. His monthly truck loan principal repayments of $300 would need to be included as a monthly cash outflow on his cash flow statement (on Line L). However, his monthly loan principal repayments are <u>not</u> included on his income statement as an expense since the principal of the loan ($18,000) is not really his money (it was merely lent to him) and so cannot be considered his expense. However, his monthly interest expense of $125 on the truck loan each month would not only be included as a monthly cash outflow (Line M), but as an expense that he incurred to earn revenue. Therefore, interest expense <u>is</u> included in his income statement (Line 8).*

- *He knew that depreciation on the truck (see Section 8A for depreciation explanation) did not involve an actual cash outflow since it was merely an accounting method to allocate the original purchase price over its useful life (remember the entire original purchase price of $18,000 was already considered as an outflow in Month 1, Line K). Therefore, <u>depreciation would not be included in a cash flow statement</u> (but since it was an expense incurred in operating the business it was included in the income statement on Line 10).*

Delayed receipt of cash can strain your cash flow.

The abbreviated four-month cash flow statement on the next page (the complete income statement and cash flow appears in the Appendix E **Financial Example**) shows Lightcost Lighting the importance of projecting its cash flow. The profit and loss statement recorded a profit for Month 1 of $125 (Line 13 Net Profit) while the cash flow statement shows a cash *deficit* of $2300 (Month 1, Line U). Note that this deficit becomes the *opening cash balance* for Month 2 (Line A) allowing for a running total of the cash position. This cash shortage for Lightcost Lighting results from the time delay in receiving actual cash from customers while having to pay suppliers and other ongoing expenses. The cash amounts that are not collected at the time of sale are known as *accounts receivable* since they are *received* at some time in the future.

If you follow the collection of the cash from the Month 1 $2500 sale (Line B) through Month 2 to Month 4 (see circled numbers forming a stepped pattern on Lines D, E, and F) you can see that the entire amount is eventually collected but it takes a total of 90 days (or 3 full months) after the sale to receive it all. A similar pattern is also apparent for the Month 2 estimated sales of $2500. If you need to clarify this further, take any month's sales figure (in the full cash flow in Appendix E) and follow it using a stepped pattern similar to the circled numbers you will see that each sales total is collected in full *but not until 90 days after the month-end has passed.*

To cover these shortages caused by the delays Philip, the owner, can use his own personal money and put it into the company, or he can approach a lender such as a bank, to obtain an *operating line of credit* for his business to cover *operating expenses*. A operating line is simply a set amount of money that is

LIGHTCOST LIGHTING PROJECTED INCOME STATEMENT Month 1-Month 4 , Year 1

		MONTH			
		1	2	3	4
1	**Sales**	**2500**	**2500**	**7500**	**10000**
2	Less cost of installers fees	700	700	2100	2800
3	Less cost of lights	300	300	900	1200
4	**TOTAL Cost of sales**	**1000**	**1000**	**3000**	**4000**
5	**Gross Profit**	**1500**	**1500**	**4500**	**6000**
	OPERATING EXPENSES				
6	Rent	300	300	300	300
7	Insurance	100	100	100	100
8	Interest	125	125	125	125
9	Advertising	400	400	400	300
10	Depreciation	375	375	375	375
11	Telephone	75	75	75	75
12	**TOTAL EXPENSES**	**1375**	**1375**	**1375**	**1275**
13	**NET PROFIT**	**125**	**125**	**3125**	**4725**

LIGHTCOST LIGHTING PROJECTED CASH FLOW STATEMENT Month 1- Month 4, Year 1

		1	2	3	4
A	**Opening Cash Balance**	**0**	**-2300**	**-3850**	**-6150**
B	**Estimated Sales**	**2500**	**2500**	**7500**	**10000**
	CASH INFLOWS				
C	Cash Sales (0%)	0	0	0	0
D	Collection of Acc. Rec. due in 30 days (30%)	0	750	750	2250
E	Collection of Acc. Rec. due in 60 days (50%)	0	0	1250	1250
F	Collection of Acc. Rec. due in 90 days (20%)	0	0	0	500
G	Total Cash Collected from Sales	0	750	2000	4000
H	Truck Loan Proceeds Received	18000	0	0	0
I	Total Cash Received	18000	750	2000	4000
J	**Total Available Cash (A + I)**	**18000**	**-1550**	**-1850**	**-2150**
	CASH OUTFLOWS				
K	Purchase of Truck	18000	0	0	0
L	Truck Loan Principal Loan Payment	300	300	300	300
M	Truck Loan Interest on Payment	125	125	125	125
N	Installers Fees ($700 per floor)	700	700	2100	2800
O	Cost of lights ($300 per floor)	300	300	900	1200
P	Rent	300	300	300	300
Q	Insurance	100	100	100	100
R	Advertising	400	400	400	300
S	Telephone	75	75	75	75
T	**Total Outflows**	**20300**	**2300**	**4300**	**5200**
U	**Closing Cash Balance (J-T)**	**-2300**	**-3850**	**-6150**	**-7350**

Note: Monthly Closing Cash Balance becomes next month's Opening Cash Balance

available for occasional short-term needs and is paid back from sales revenues. Some typical situations requiring operating lines include businesses who sell mostly on credit to be paid sometime in the future or businesses that have large inventory levels (such as a toy store prior to Christmas). For those selling on credit, there is always a risk that a customer will never pay. Therefore, it is important to ensure that your customer is reliable before granting credit (a credit check on any new customers can be done by your bank as discussed in Section 6C **Order Processing**). Carrying high inventory levels requires large cash outlays to maintain and also exposes you to the potential risk that change in product style or customer preference can render the inventory unsellable which can further harm your cash flow. Therefore, close monitoring of your inventory is very important (see Section 6E **Inventory**).

Many businesses use operating lines as a normal course of business and it is not necessarily a sign of weakness to require one. However, it is extremely important for a business to collect its accounts receivable as quickly as possible since this will minimize usage of an operating line and the associated interest costs. It is similar to using a credit card to pay your expenses while waiting for your weekly pay. Philip could help his situation by telling the installation company that it would be paid only when he was paid, and bargaining with the lighting materials supplier for more time to make payments (such as terms of 60 days to better match his receipts of payment from his own customers). The combination of delaying the payment of expenses as long as possible and trying to collect receivables as soon as possible

The Idea Guide

(see section 6C **Order Processing**) minimizes the potential shortages in cash flow that lead to high usage of a credit line. However, your ability to demand these terms largely depends on the availability of alternate suppliers (see Section 6B **Suppliers**) and how many alternative products your customers have available (see section 4A **Competitors**).

Looking at the four-month cash flow statement, Lightcost Lighting would require an operating line of approximately $7500 (Month 4, Line U is the maximum shortage at $7350) to cover its cash deficit over the first few months. A bank would evaluate what amount of operating line Lightcost Lighting would receive by how well-prepared and realistic the income statement and cash flow statement were. Therefore, it is important to lay out all of your realistic assumptions just as Philip did in this example. Another factor is how reliable the bank perceives the customers of Lightcost Lighting to be in terms of paying what they owe since these payments will become the cash to repay Lightcost's loan (the bank may do a credit check on the business customers of Lightcost to see if they have a clean record of paying previous suppliers). However, the bank would first evaluate the rest of the plan (denoted by the previous steps in *The Idea Guide*) to see if it makes sense before referring to the financial statements and clientele payment history.

> **Cash Flow Statements account for every dollar that flows into and out of the business.**

Planning Questions 8B

1. What percentage of your total sales will you collect immediately? What percentage of your total sales will be collected in 30, 45, 60, 90 or 120 days (you first addressed this in Section 6C **Order Processing** question 2)? Consider the norm for your type of business.

IMMEDIATE COLLECTION	30 DAY COLLECTION	45 DAY COLLECTION	60 DAY COLLECTION	90 DAY COLLECTION	120 DAY COLLECTION
%	%	%	%	%	%

2. To begin a cash flow statement, refer to the blank column on the far left of your income statement worksheet on page 78. Insert the number of days that payment for each expense is due after the expense is incurred. For items such as rent, which are due in the month that they are incurred, insert 0 (zero). You likely have variable expense components to your cost of sales as TJ's Specialty Coffee Shop did. If so, list on the table below the approximate cost each time the item is purchased from a supplier, and how much time you have to pay a supplier for it. For TJ's this could be sugar that is purchased in amounts of $50 monthly in the quiet season and $75 in the busy season and must be paid within 30 days after delivery from a supplier. Conversely, Lightcost Lighting purchased all of its supplies as the job occurred (lights and installer services) with no time period allowed for payment.

VARIABLE ITEM PURCHASES

VARIABLE ITEMS	AMOUNT PURCHASED EACH TIME ($)	WHEN DUE (30 days, 60 days)	HOW MANY TIMES per MONTH?

3. Begin constructing a cash flow statement by transferring your income statement items to the cash flow statement worksheet provided below. Remember to take into account your time assumptions made in questions 1 and 2 above (also explained in Section 8E **Assumptions**). Remember also to include any disbursements for equipment (and a source for the cash) and any related loan and interest repayments. Refer to the Lightcost Lighting example (pages 79-81) for guidance.

MONTHLY CASH FLOW WORKSHEET

							Months						
	1	2	3	4	5	6	7	8	9	10	11	12	Total
A Opening Cash Balance													
CASH INFLOWS													
B Estimated Sales													
C													
D Cash Sales (%)													
E Collection 30 day A/R (%)													
F Collection 60 day A/R (%)													
G Collection 90 day A/R (%)													
H Total Collected From Sales D+E+F+G													
I Loans Proceeds Received													
J Total Cash Inflows (H+I)													
CASH OUTFLOWS													
K Principal Loan Repayments													
L Loan Interest Repayment													
M													
N													
O													
P													
Q													
R													
S													
T Total Outflows (sum K to S)													
U Closing Cash Balance (J-T)													

Evaluator's Thoughts

Cash flow projections are important for evaluators such as banks. Banks want to see that the business has thought about the cash implications of its operations and that there will be enough cash generated to pay back loans and interest. Cash flow projections also allow you to prepare ahead of time for any shortages that you may incur. Do not be afraid to show a shortage as this is why you are at the bank seeking money. However, nothing is more devastating to a business' credibility as showing up to ask a lender for an operating line *after* the shortage has actually occurred, since it shows a lack of preparation.

8C BREAK-EVEN POINT: What amount of sales covers your costs?

To determine how many sales you will need to break-even in your first year, all your costs must first be considered. As mentioned previously, costs can come in two forms, *variable expenses* that vary with sales and other operating or *fixed expenses* that do not vary according to sales. You have already done all of the necessary preparation to do a *break-even analysis*. A summary of the steps in a break-even calculation appear below.

1. Note your selling price.
2. Note the total of your variable expenses per unit (which is your *total cost of sale per unit* arrived at in Section 8A Planning Question 2).
3. Note the *yearly* total of your other operating expenses (fixed expenses) which are appropriate for your projected level of sales volume (calculated in section 8A Planning Question 4).

Example

Philip determined that Lightcost Lighting would charge approximately $2500 per floor. His variable expenses of $300 (lights) and $700 (installation company's fees) created a total cost of goods sold of $1000. His fixed expenses will total $15,400 for the year (see the total projected operating expenses on the Lightcost Lighting Income statement in Appendix E).

$$\textbf{Break-even Number of Units} = \frac{\textbf{Total Operating Expenses}}{\textbf{Price-Variable Expenses per Unit}}$$

$$= \frac{\$15,400}{\$2500 - \$1000}$$

$$= 10.26 \text{ units}$$

Philip must sell 10.26 projects to break-even. Using the unit selling price, this translates into 10.26 x $2500 (selling price) or $25,650 in yearly sales for Philip to break-even.

Philip could also do his break-even in another way. He knows that he will try to get at least a 60% margin on everything he sells (see how he arrived at this in the Example in Section 5E **Pricing**). He also knows that the gross margin that he makes will be used to cover the rest of his operating expenses. He can then calculate his break-even sales revenue requirement. Businesses that sell more than one type of product often use this gross margin percentage method to determine their break-even point.

$$\textbf{Break-even Sales Revenue} = \frac{\textbf{Total Operating Expenses}}{\textbf{Gross Profit Margin \%}}$$

$$= \frac{\$15,400}{60\%}$$

$$= \frac{15,400}{.60} = \$25,666$$

Philip would require $25,666 in sales of lighting projects to break-even (the small difference from the previous break-even of $25,650 is due to rounding).

Although operating expenses not related to each unit of product sold are referred to as fixed expenses, they can change with various levels of sales. For example, an increase in business volume may necessitate more maintenance to repair equipment or the hiring of an extra employee to handle the increase. This is important because your break-even analysis is based on an assumption that your costs are for a certain range of sales that you believe is realistic (see the first paragraph in the Section 8A). Therefore, if you want to see what your break-even point would be at a substantially higher volume of sales, you should first consider whether your operating expenses would also need to increase before doing the calculation.

A break-even calculation may indicate that you need excessive and unrealistic sales volume to reach a break-even point. If this is the case, there may be a few possible reasons, all of which are simple to investigate:

Changing the price Can you increase your price? Will customers still purchase? Keep in mind your target market (Section 3A **Target Market**) and what they would be willing to pay. Note that if you lower the selling price to $2000 in the previous example, the break-even amount will increase to 15 projects. The lower the price you set, the higher the break-even volume needed since you would be making less money per unit sold.

Reducing variable expenses Can you cut down some of your operation or delivery costs by improving your operations (through improved employee efficiency, less expensive delivery or commission expenses, cheaper materials, for example) without sacrificing the final product? Decreasing your variable expenses (Section 8A Planning Question 2) reduces the amount of volume you need to sell to break-even. Try changing the variable expenses in the previous example (lights and installation costs) and notice how it will change the break-even amount required.

Reducing operating expenses This can be done for fixed items such as rent and utilities, for example. Keeping fixed expenses at a minimum will improve your profitability. Perhaps rather than renting office space you can initially run your business from home. Can you put sales staff on commission rather than salary? Commissions would be considered a variable expense as they would fluctuate with the number units that are sold. There may be other operating expenses you could also reduce (see Chapter 6 **OPERATIONS**).

Other possible adjustments Can you change your marketing methods to reach more potential buyers or network with other companies to increase your sales (see Chapter 5 **MARKETING PLAN**)? Increasing your sales will make your break-even more attainable.

Planning Question 8C

1. What is your break-even number of orders and sales revenue based on your income statement projections? (Use either of the two methods discussed). Can you reduce any expenses or change your price to make your break-even point lower?

Evaluator's Thoughts

Your break-even analysis details an absolute minimum sales requirement for your business to cover its costs. This is an important part of your idea development and overall preparation because it gives an indication of how easy or difficult it would be to reach that minimum goal. If the goal is relatively easy to attain, your business proposal will seem realistic. The break-even point also allows the reader to put your estimated sales into context by seeing how far above break-even you have projected.

8D FINANCIAL RECORDS: Who will do the books?

Most individuals want to start a certain business because they like the idea, not because they like to do the bookkeeping for the idea. It is probably best for you to focus on what you do best and find others to do this function since you will be happier and the business more productive. Timely, regular compilation of financial information is a key element of business success. A bookkeeper or accountant can be hired by the hour on a monthly basis for assistance in maintaining financial information. This does not suggest that you can ignore the numbers. Ensure that whoever does the books provides you with a regular report of your income and expenses (see Section 8A **Income Statement** for details) to help you make more accurate and efficient decisions on budgeting, pricing, marketing, operations, and expenditures.

One way to stay abreast of the finances is to try to at least keep several file folders (one for each category on your income statement such as "*telephone*" or "*office supplies*") and make sure the receipts and invoices from each transaction are placed into the appropriate one. This will cut down your time and costs to organize it later and also keep you informed. These figures should be added up monthly at least for the first year. Local bank branches also have booklets or guidelines for keeping track of financial results. When an existing business with previous sales activity seeks financing, most investors or lenders require at least a yearly financial statement that has been reviewed or prepared by a professional accountant.

Maintaining financial information is essential to business success.

A balance sheet is often required to show the financial worth and health of your business at a particular moment in time. It shows business assets which are items that are owned by the business such as cash, equipment, accounts receivable (representing money owed by customers for sales on account), and so forth. It also records outstanding *liabilities* which are debts such as short-term or long-term loans, taxes, and accounts payable that the business owes to suppliers, lenders, or others. Any loan with a repayment period over a year (Lightcost Lighting's truck loan, for example) is considered a long-term loan. An operating credit line would be considered a short-term loan as it is a loan to augment temporary cashflow shortages. The third category is *owners' equity* representing money invested by the owners or portions of net profits retained in the business.

For a small business startup situation, a *projected balance sheet* would show the worth of the business in the future. A projected balance sheet is not always necessary unless the business is extremely complicated or possesses many expensive assets. However, most established businesses should prepare a balance sheet at the end of their first year. To determine the value of assets on the balance sheet, for example, information from your income statement (net profits and depreciation), your cash flow (cash balance, outstanding accounts receivable due from customers and other items), and your original value of assets will be used. Therefore, it is important to retain receipts showing details of every transaction. To prepare a balance sheet that properly reflects your business operations, a professional accountant may be best suited to assist you. However, you can minimize the time required and the corresponding costs by receiving a running total of your monthly income and expenses on an income statement and through receipts of every transaction. An example of the Lightcost Lighting Balance Sheet appears in Appendix E **Financial Example**.

Planning Question 8D

1. Who is responsible for financial record keeping? What is their qualification or experience? Outline how you will ensure regular monitoring of financial results?

Evaluator's Thoughts

When a business becomes involved in its daily operations, it is easy to forget the importance of maintaining financial records for every transaction. If an evaluator has invested in or lent money to a business, they will require periodic financial information such as an income statement. Considering how you plan to maintain financial monitoring of the business will help you address this important area.

8E ASSUMPTIONS: How did you derive your figures?

Predictions are rarely 100% accurate but, when based on realistic assumptions, help give you an idea of the future. When constructing projected statements for a future time period, it is important to state how certain figures were derived unless it is very obvious. These assumptions create a foundation to assist you in building your financial statements. Refer to TJ's Specialty Coffee Shop (pages 74-75) and Lightcost Lighting (pages 76-80) for assumption examples on income and cash flow statements.

Planning Question 8E

1. List the assumptions for the items on your projected income statement and cash flow statement.

Evaluator's Thoughts

Since an evaluator will only see a finished projected income and cash flow statement, simple and clear assumptions are necessary for them to understand how the numbers (sales figures, expenses, timing of collection of cash from sales) were derived. Your financial statements should have a letter or number reference on lines (see Lightcost Lighting cash flow example in this chapter) representing rows of figures that may require further explanation. Assumptions listed below and corresponding to these line numbers are excellent explanatory tools and give the evaluator the impression that you are up front and not "hiding behind" numbers. Simple assumptions are particularly important if your business idea is a not a well-known type of operation or is technically complicated.

8F FINANCIAL REQUIREMENTS: What do you need and why?

In Section 6K **Cost of Operations** you made note of your initial expenditures on such things as initial inventory, equipment, and other expenditures commonly called *capital purchases*. Also, included in Section 6K were other miscellaneous initial costs such as office supplies or phones. These are your *startup costs* which you can either pay for yourself or, alternatively, try to finance with a loan which you will repay with the cash your business generates (hence, the importance of a cash flow statement). The cash flow projections in Section 8B showed you the cash shortages that may occur on a periodic basis in your business. These are your *ongoing short-term operating needs* (sometimes called "*working capital*" requirements). These ongoing needs are different from startup costs. If you run a cash business, you likely will not need an operating line of credit. However, if you are not paid immediately by customers (as in the Lightcost Lighting example in this chapter), you may need an operating line of credit to purchase more inventory, pay employees, and fulfill other daily obligations.

SOURCES OF FUNDS

LOANS
- Loans from institutions or individuals
- Government Assistance
- Suppliers (credit terms)

EQUITY
(in return for share of ownership or profits)
- Personal savings
- Relatives
- Cash from partners
- Venture capital companies
- Investors

The Idea Guide

Planning Questions 8F

1. Refer back to Section 6K **Cost of Operations** (questions 6 and 7). List your initial costs to purchase necessary assets (equipment, furniture, fixtures, building renovations etc.) and how much you will contribute to the cost. The balance will need to be lent for by a lender or investor.

INITIAL CAPITAL PURCHASES

ITEM	COST	YOUR CONTRIBUTION	BALANCE REQUIRED
BUILDING			
EQUIPMENT/VEHICLES			
TOTAL			

2. Refer back to 6K **Cost of Operations** (questions 5 and 9) and note the short-term needs that you must purchase before you start your business (such as purchase of inventory or office supplies). These should also appear in Month 1 of your cash flow projections as they are considered part of your short-term requirements.

INITIAL CASH REQUIREMENT (AMOUNT)

3. Refer to your projected cash flow statement completed in Planning Questions 8B and identify which month contains your maximum cash deficit. An operating credit line may be necessary to help you meet this deficit and by identifying this maximum amount, you will ensure that can cover any other month's shortfall. Alternatively, you can choose to cover this maximum cash flow deficit or ongoing periodic shortfalls with your own money.

ONGOING MAXIMUM OPERATING REQUIREMENT (AMOUNT)	MONTH

Evaluator's Thoughts

This section helps you see your requirements more clearly. This will allow you to plan in terms of time required to obtain the amounts of money and the resources available to provide these funds (including your own savings as a possibility). If you are approaching an evaluator, the preparation of initial and ongoing requirements also show that a business has thought about and summarized its future needs. The evaluator will analyze whether the requirements seem excessive or fall short of what your particular type of business would seem to require. Inclusion of loan and interest repayments in future periods of the projected cash flow statement will demonstrate to the evaluator that you are capable of repaying amounts borrowed. The evaluator may also be interested in what percentage of the initial requirements the owner would finance through their own personal resources. Use of some personal resources demonstrates commitment and confidence in the business idea and is often a requirement if you ask a bank for a loan.

9 GOALS AND OBJECTIVES:

The Timing For Future Events

You have thought about a great deal of important information regarding planning a business and considered how it relates to your own plan by answering the questions. You have most of the material you need; now it's a matter of setting a time frame for gathering any missing information or finalizing details of the information you have recorded. This section allows you to set some future objectives and deadlines for finishing your plan. These could include setting a deadline for finding out any missing costs of your product, talking to potential suppliers, determining your location, or inventory needs, and so on. If you are finished, this section can be used to identify any major events that will likely occur in the future such as leasing a location, starting dates, expanding the business, offering new products, and so forth. Setting objectives will challenge you and keep you in a motivated, thinking mode.

Example

Diana knows that to finish her plans for the clothing store Accessory Room (original example in Section 3A), she needs to gather or finalize some details. This includes considering a suitable location once she determines her inventory requirements, determining her employee needs, and establishing a hiring criteria. She must also evaluate and choose between supplier alternatives. Finally, she must do a projected income and cash flow statement once she finalizes the costs associated with these issues. Completing these items will allow Diana to fairly evaluate her idea.

Planning Questions 9

1. Refer to the chart representing each section of the guide. Determine whether you have completed the section thoroughly. You can keep updating this table as you finalize each section to give you a record of where you stand.

	PLANNING ITEM	COMPLETE		PLANNING ITEM	COMPLETE		PLANNING ITEM	COMPLETE
1A	OWNERS	☐Yes ☐No	5A	MARKETING MESSAGE	☐Yes ☐No	6J	SUCCESS FACTORS	☐Yes ☐No
2A	PRODUCT /SERVICE	☐Yes ☐No	5B	MARKETING MIX	☐Yes ☐No	6K	COST OF OPERATIONS	☐Yes ☐No
2B	BASIC REQUIREMENT	☐Yes ☐No	5C	DISTRIBUTION	☐Yes ☐No	7A	MANAGEMENT TEAM	☐Yes ☐No
2C	LEGAL ISSUES	☐Yes ☐No	5D	MARKETING BUDGET	☐Yes ☐No	7B	PERSONNEL	☐Yes ☐No
3A	TARGET MARKET	☐Yes ☐No	5E	PRICING	☐Yes ☐No	7C	ADVISORS	☐Yes ☐No
3B	MARKET AREA	☐Yes ☐No	5F	SALES OBJECTIVE	☐Yes ☐No	7D	FUTURE ISSUES	☐Yes ☐No
3C	MARKET SIZE	☐Yes ☐No	6A	LOCATION	☐Yes ☐No	7E	COMPENSATION	☐Yes ☐No
3D	SPEC.CONSIDERATIONS	☐Yes ☐No	6B	SUPPLIERS	☐Yes ☐No	8A	INCOME STATEMENT	☐Yes ☐No
3E	MKT. ENVIRONMENT	☐Yes ☐No	6C	ORDER PROCESSING	☐Yes ☐No	8B	CASH FLOW STATE.	☐Yes ☐No
3F	FUTURE TRENDS	☐Yes ☐No	6D	HANDLING	☐Yes ☐No	8C	BREAK-EVEN POINT	☐Yes ☐No
4A	COMPETITORS	☐Yes ☐No	6E	INVENTORY	☐Yes ☐No	8D	FINANCIAL RECORDS	☐Yes ☐No
4B	COMPET. ADVANTAGE	☐Yes ☐No	6F	EQUIPMENT	☐Yes ☐No	8E	ASSUMPTIONS	☐Yes ☐No
4C	COMPET. RESPONSE	☐Yes ☐No	6G	CAPACITY	☐Yes ☐No	8F	FIN. REQUIREMENTS	☐Yes ☐No
4D	BARRIERS TO ENTRY	☐Yes ☐No	6H	INFORMATION	☐Yes ☐No	9	GOALS & OBJECTIVES	☐Yes ☐No
4E	MARKET SHARE	☐Yes ☐No	6I	ENVIRONMENT	☐Yes ☐No	10	SUMMARY	☐Yes ☐No

2. Refer to the chart in the previous question and list the sections that remain incomplete. For each section, identify the required information (or required actions) that must be addressed to complete the section and the date by which each piece of missing information will be gathered. In the third column, set a deadline for yourself by which time the section must be completed. Keep in mind that some issues (location, for example) may require you to consider other issues (amount of inventory) prior to finalizing.

INCOMPLETE SECTION	NATURE OF REQUIRED DETAILS AND WHEN THEY WILL BE ADDRESSED	TIME FRAME TO FINALIZE

3. Are there any other issues that do not appear on the table in question 1 which are keeping you from completing the plan? What can you do about this (take a course, read a book, attend an entrepreneurial seminar, etc.)? When will you resolve these issues?

4. When do you see your venture beginning? Keep in mind that you may require substantial time between completing your plan and starting the business (time required to sign a lease, hire employees, attain financing, complete renovations, etc.).

Evaluator's Thoughts

Businesses that set objectives have a better chance of future success than those that simply have vague ideas of the future. This is true for a business in both its planning stages and after it has started operating. In either case, evaluators look to see that a business owner has motivation in the form of future objectives. For an established business, this can include higher sales or profitability objectives. Objectives could also be events that will change or expand the business such as future products, new territories, and so on. For a startup, this includes the sequence of events that must be addressed for startup to occur. Both scenarios are most clearly communicated when dates are included to give a sense of when exactly the items will occur.

10 SUMMARY:

A Concise Description Of Your Idea

You are now at the final stage of gathering information - except for the fact that there is nothing left to gather. This short chapter involves simply summarizing the key points of your plan. Everything you need to summarize (the idea, the resources that you possess and the requirements for going forward) has been addressed in the questions in each section. Why do you need a summary? It provides you with a quick, concise description of your idea when interested customers, partners, or other evaluators ask you to explain what it is you are doing. You should be able to concisely describe your idea in one page by summarizing the main points from the sections listed in the side box. These sections represent the common key sections for both product or service businesses. Keep in mind that other sections may be relevant for your particular type of business such as Section 6A **Location** (for retail stores), or 2C **Legal Issues** (patent, franchise, or liability issues).

MAIN SECTIONS FOR SUMMARY

1A Owners	3E Market Environment
1B Developments to Date	4A Competitors
2A Product/Service Details	4B Competitive Advantage
3A Target Market	5F Sales Objectives
3B Market Area	8A Income Statement
3C Potential Market Size	9 Goals and Objectives

Example

SUMMARY: DIANA'S ACCESSORY ROOM (original example in Section 3A **Target Market**)

- *Accessory Room, a retail clothing store, will be started this fall by Diana who has four years experience within a retail environment.* (information from Section 1A **Owners**)

- *The store will sell mid-priced clothing and accessories aimed primarily at working women.* (from Section 2A **Product/Service Details**)

- *The target market is young, female, and employed and requires stylish, reasonably priced clothes for weekends and casual office wear.* (Section 3A **Target Market**)

- *The store will serve the local area market which has a target market female population of 3,000 within a 30 mile radius of the store.* (Section 3B **Market Location** and 3C **Potential Market Size**)

- *The trend of casual dress in the workplace is an opportunity for the Accessory Room as women seek clothes that are appropriate in a less formal environment while retaining a look of professionalism.* (Section 3E **Market Environment**)

- *Competition is limited for this segment as most of the stores in the area carry merchandise*

The Idea Guide

for all ages and styles (such as large department stores) or carry unisex clothes geared to young males and females. Accessory Room's competitive advantage is its stylish, reasonably priced clothing and accessories for the young female. (Section 4A **Competitor**s and 4B **Competitive Advantage**)

- *The store will be located in downtown Mapleton, a popular regional shopping zone for the surrounding area.* (Section 6A **Location**)

- *Arrangements have been made with several suppliers of reasonably priced fashionable clothing and accessories.* (Section 1B **Developments to Date** or Section 6B **Suppliers**)

- *Accessory Room has sales objectives of $30,000 for its first year of operations, $38,000 in Year 2, and $44,000 in year 3. Net profit for Year 1 is projected at $15,000, Year 2 at $20,000, and Year 3 at $24,000.* (Section 5F **Sales Objective** and 8A **Income Statement**)

- *Accessory Room is seeking financing of $10,000 for initial startup costs related to purchase of initial inventory and fixtures and an ongoing operating credit line of $5,000.* (Chapter 9 **Goals and Objectives** and Section 8F **Financial Requirements**).

NOTE: Section references like those appearing in the parentheses above are not necessary and are included for demonstrative purposes only. If you are seeking financing from the evaluator, include your financial requirements as demonstrated in this example.

Planning Question 10

1. Summarize the key sections of your plan in one or two sentences each using the sections outlined in the box above. While these sections are the ones that all businesses have in common, keep in mind that your particular business may have additional key sections not mentioned above (i.e., in the example Diana used *location* and *suppliers* because they are additional key elements to a retail business, while an inventor or franchisee may discuss legal issues in respect to patents or franchises).

Evaluator's Thoughts

When you provide a written summary of the idea to a potential evaluator it gives them a quick grasp of what the business idea is all about before getting into its details. This allows them to see where your plan is headed by putting the details of each section of the plan into a larger perspective as they read through it. Plans without a summary remain somewhat ambiguous to an evaluator since they can be difficult to follow. Also, summaries are commonplace between business professionals who may lack the necessary time to read an entire document. Since evaluators, in particular, may be busy reviewing a number of proposals at any one time, they appreciate those plans that attempt to help them quickly and clearly understand through use of a quick summary. Including a summary will demonstrate both your sophistication and recognition of an evaluator's viewpoint. It is also an excellent way to attract attention for your idea since it creates a natural curiosity to read the entire plan. Because a summary provides a reader with a quick explanation before they read the rest of your plan, it should appear at the very beginning (after a title page and before a table of contents) in your finished plan.

CONCLUSION

Going Forward with Your Idea

When someone has thought so thoroughly about a business idea, they probably wonder what else they can do to move forward. The first thing to do is to congratulate yourself. You set an objective to get through this book and you've done it. To go through such a comprehensive process has to make you feel good since the information has finally been taken from the inside of your head and and begun to shape on paper.

Leave the guide alone for awhile and play with your idea even if you are still unsure about it. The first thing to do is be positive and keeping jotting notes down to yourself. Jotting down these notes will spawn more ideas to help fill in some gaps that may remain. Think of signs, logos, or names that can create an image for your business. It's fun to do and keeps you motivated. Entrepreneurial exhibits and seminars are great places to meet others like yourself who can provide you with contacts, advice, or feedback.

Remember to keep your eyes open to observe other businesses and how they go about their marketing, operations, and staffing for do's and don'ts that can be incorporated or avoided in your idea. You make purchasing decisions every day. What influences you to choose one purchase over another? Can you take these lessons learned from your own purchasing decisions to influence a potential customer to choose you over a competing business.

Show the idea to friends and family who may provide you with some common sense solutions to some of the issues that are still not clear in your mind. If they react positively, ask them why. It might give a clue to another possible selling feature or potential market that you overlooked. If someone expresses doubt, try to see if you can convince them otherwise by using the wealth of information you have recorded in this guide. If you cannot, make sure that you ask them to spell out exactly what makes them doubt it. By making others spell out their concerns, you have something to take back with you and consider rather than vague feedback. This constructive criticism will only help you make your idea stronger by helping you address issues that perhaps you overlooked.

After reading this guide you know all of the necessary business terminology you will ever have to face so read up on other businesses in entrepreneurial magazines and business magazines. It will spark ideas in you and also possibly provide a key ingredient for your business.

Also, get out into the marketplace and evaluate how your business (as you have planned it) would compare to others. This will refresh your memory and reinforce why you came up with the idea in the first place. Research your needs and start coming up with options and alternatives (for suppliers, locations, marketing promotions, and so forth).

In the Appendix C: **Creating a Written Plan From Your Answers** there are some tips on writing up the plan to show your idea to prospective partners, banks, managers, and others who will be key figures in your business. Everything you need to start and run a successful business is within these pages and it all relates to your idea. Keep it around as a handbook to remind you of the important areas to manage once you start your business. By referring to it periodically, you can perform a quick diagnostic on a particular area of your business.

NOTES

APPENDIX A:

How To Gather Information

Gathering information for your idea is easy to do and crucial to evaluating your idea fairly and developing it further. Much of the information will come from inside your head since the business idea was likely yours. Additional information can come from conversations with suppliers, buyers, and competitors who can provide missing details to the various areas of your plan. Several methods are listed below.

Observational Method Posing as a customer of a competitor's business provides direct feedback on "do's and don'ts" in your own plan. Perhaps they only serve a certain territory or clientele. Is the competitor maximizing on the potential for the idea or can you spot an opportunity that they are not addressing? Would you be interested in shortening your preparation time by contacting them to become an exclusive distributor or franchisee in your area, rather than starting from scratch? Ideas for improving your own idea can be picked up observing any and all businesses with which you come in contact (while shopping, for example).

Local Library Books or periodicals on topics related to the idea can provide you with background information. In the bibliography of many books and articles are more books on the topic. The advent of on-line computers allows for quick reference of an incredible amount of subject material from newspaper articles, magazines, and books. Librarians are extremely knowledgeable and are a valuable asset in gathering any required information for any type of business idea.

Contact Industry Associations There may be an industry organization that represents companies related to your product. These associations are usually able to provide general information on the industry including notice of any workshops, seminars, or reading material on the subject.

Prospective Buyers Who knows better about what you should offer than a prospective buyer of your product/service? Prospective buyers can often provide information on pricing, needed products or services, competitors, persuasive marketing methods, and so on. They may also reveal an area of the market currently not served, or end up referring you to other potential customers.

Government Federal and other levels of governments can offer information on necessary permits, licences, zoning requirements, labour regulations, taxes, health and safety standards, exporting information, and any other pertinent information. Most federal governments have departments that gather statistics on households, industries, and other trends that can help you determine whether your idea is addressing a trend in the marketplace. Local municipalities often carry similar local information at city hall. Most levels of government, including local levels, have departments devoted specifically to supporting small business development (see listings in box at side).

> **Canadian Government Small Business Assistance**
> Business Development Bank of Canada(BDC)
> Tel: 1-888-INFO-BDC Toll-free
>
> Will identify appropriate government
> programs and BDC offices in your area.
>
> **USA Government Small Business Assistance**
> Small Business Administration (SBA)
> Tel: 1-800-827-5722 Toll-free
>
> Will identify appropriate government
> programs and SBA offices in your area.

Other Sources Local or regional chambers of commerce contain a variety of businesses and offer seminars, reading material, and economic information. Associations specifically devoted to small business development possess a wide variety of resources for the prospective business owner on issues such as marketing, exporting, and accounting (see listings below). Self-employed acquaintances or contacts in law, banking, accounting, marketing, or industries related to your business idea are helpful contacts when gathering, organizing, and presenting information. **Also, check out The Idea Guide Website for more helpful information (http://www.ideaguide.com).**

APPENDIX B:

The Uses of Your Plan

BENEFITS OF A BUSINESS PLAN

- Creates a comprehensive to-do list
- Identifies possible opportunities and risks for which a business can prepare
- Provides a blueprint to build a business
- Establishes objectives and allows for tracking of growth against initial objectives
- Introduces the company to prospective partners, distributors, and clients
- Helps establish a unified company direction for employees and management
- Clearly defines or delegates responsibilities
- Educates new employees and managers
- Attracts investment capital and bank financing

Organizing the business idea into a written plan provides a prospective business owner with several benefits (see side box for some of these benefits).

The last benefit on the list could be the most important one if you need to find sources of financing to support your idea. Businesses do not necessarily require financing to establish. However, when they do require financial assistance, they are subject to a thorough evaluation by the lending individual or bank. The reason for needing thorough information is illustrated by a simple example. Suppose that you have been entrusted with a friend's money. If a third person were to approach you about borrowing this money, chances are you would be extremely cautious. You would probably ask:

- How is this third person going to repay and when?
- Has the person borrowed from others in the past and were these individuals repaid?
- For what purpose is the money to be used?
- Does the purpose make sense or is there a risk that the money will be lost and not repaid?

When you approach a bank or investor, *you* are the third person trying to borrow *their* friend's money (customer savings deposits and investments). People often have the misconception that banks lend their own money or that banks are financed by the government. Banks are lending out their *customers'* money and make a profit by making a *spread* (difference) between what they offer on a savings account and what they charge for a loan. Since the money used to provide loans comes from bank customers (called *depositors*), the number one priority of any bank is to safeguard these funds since at any time depositors can demand their money back. Given this priority the banks are not interested in any loan perceived as risky. Another misconception is that collateral alone should be good enough to support any loan request. However, collateral in the form of assets such as equipment, vehicles, inventory, and buildings loses much of its value in the event that a bank must seize the items and try to sell them. This is why bankruptcy sales and auctions have such good selling prices. Therefore, collateral is usually inadequate to cover the loan amount. In addition, the time, expense, and administration in seizing assets makes reliance on collateral alone not worth the trouble.

Banks fear risk: lack of a plan suggests potential risk.

Rather than relying on collateral when lending, banks rely on choosing loan applicants with sound proposals. Sound proposals suggest the ability to repay. Therefore, business loan proposals that are *not* communicated effectively because of inadequate information signify an unacceptable level of risk and likely will not gain an evaluator's support. This is because they have not fully addressed the last of the bullet points above (purpose of loan making sense). You can directly address this fear of risk by presentation of an organized written plan such as the one that this guide allows you to prepare.

As mentioned above, banks take the difference between the savings deposit rate (for example, 4%) and the loan rate (for example, 7%) to earn a spread (3% in this case). However, they only typically make 1% profit on the total amount borrowed (after paying related expenses such as administration, staffing etc.). Using this minimal typical 1% profit, the importance of addressing the bank's fear of risk can be illustrated with an example.

> **Banks must guess correctly on 99.5% of their loans.**

Example 1

A bank lends out $10,000 of its depositors' money to a business. The loan is successfully repaid. Due to bank overhead, administrative time, and monitoring of the loan, the bank makes 1% on its money. Therefore profit in this case is $10,000 x 1% = $100

Example 2

A startup business owner approaches a bank without a written business plan and is denied a loan of $10,000. The bank manager explains that the bank does not understand enough about the proposed business to lend out its depositors' money. The bank manager demonstrates to the business owner the ramifications of what would happen if the business was unable to repay the $10,000. If this occurred, not only would the bank not earn its 1% return on the $10,000 ($100), but the entire loan amount ($10,000) is also lost. Therefore, the bank must give out enough new loans to recover the $10,000 that would be lost. The bank manager explains that since only 1% return is made on any loan, the bank would have to lend out new loans totalling $1 million to earn the 1% return sufficient to recover the lost $10,000.

$10,000/1%=New Loans Required to Recover Losses
$10,000/.01=$1 million

Therefore, the bank will not entertain the business owner's request until they understand more about the business idea, suggesting a written business plan that describes the potential idea, market, competition, marketing, operations, and personnel.

As you can probably guess from this example, banks are not interested in lending to businesses that fail to communicate the nature of their activities since this would imply risk to the funds that have been deposited in the bank by customers. This is validated by the fact that banks traditionally project to lose only 1/2 of 1% of their loans meaning banks must guess correctly on 99.5% of all money that is lent. This slim margin for error, in turn, results in close scrutiny of each potential loan. Similarly, investors do not like losing their money (commonly referred to as "*capital*"). Therefore, those startups that can demonstrate convincingly that their business is of acceptable risk will acquire money more easily and at lower interest rates (since a bank's perceived risk of the venture influences the loan rate).

The most effective way to do this is to prepare a written plan (like you have done in this book) that clearly lays out all aspects of your business idea so that an evaluator can see that the risk is acceptable. A complete plan on paper provides the impression that you are serious, confident, well-prepared, and ready to begin. It can influence a bank or other evaluator to take your proposal seriously and support it. Loan applicants that fail to provide a written plan are usually forced to prepare one to even be considered. However, the fact that individuals need to be told by a bank or investor to provide a written business plan for such a major undertaking is a serious blow to the individual's credibility as an able business person. Various estimates have been made that suggest that upwards of 60-70% of those approaching a bank neglect to provide a written plan and, consequently, do not attain financing. Therefore, individuals with a clearly laid out plan such as the one outlined in this guide are immediately head-and-shoulders above all other applicants.

APPENDIX **C**:

Creating A Written Plan From Your Answers

You can turn the information that you have assembled into a formal business plan suitable for your future reference and any evaluator's purposes. Here are a few guidelines to follow:

C1 CONTENTS OF YOUR PLAN: What needs to be included?

Chapters The headings of each chapter will become the major chapters in your written plan. Insert only the first part of the chapter titles. For example, "THE BUSINESS: General Information on You and Your Idea" would become THE BUSINESS since the rest would confuse a reader of your plan.

Subsections The subsections in each chapter can similarly be adjusted by inserting the upper case portion of the section titles rather than the entire title for the same reason as above. For example, the Section 3A title on page 12 of the guide will appear on your written plan as "TARGET MARKET" instead of "Who will buy your product?" You can use a similar numbering system of 3A, 3B, etc.

SOME SUPPORTING DOCUMENTS

- supplier list
- customer list
- distributors
- patents
- trademarks
- accountants
- related news articles
- photographs of product
- copy of sales contracts
- franchise agreements
- licensing agreements
- manager resumes

Sentences Simply rewrite the answers to the questions into complete sentences. The questions have been placed in sequential order to allow you to have coherent sentences and paragraphs that build on one another to effectively describe each section of the business. The **FINANCIAL** section (Chapter 8) need not contain any sentences other than the list of assumptions used in coming up with some of the numbers (see 8E **Assumptions**).

Table Of Contents Identify each chapter, subsection within a chapter, and any appendices by a table of contents to allow a reader to flip quickly to a certain section.

Supporting Documents (Appendices) Throughout this guide the importance of supporting evidence was reinforced. This evidence can be placed as appendices in your finished plan which will help a reader who wants to investigate a point further. When you mention a point for which you have a related magazine article or statistics to help illustrate, refer the reader to the appendix for the actual source. These items give a sense of legitimacy to your idea. These could include items such as related news articles, photographs or computer illustrations of products, a list of sales contracts successfully achieved, a list of involved persons/managers/advisors or companies (clients, accountants, lawyers, suppliers, distributors, and so on), any franchise/licensing agreements, documentation of any patents or trademarks, and so forth.

Introductory Letter A covering letter helps introduce your business idea and outlines exactly what you are looking for from the reader. You may be looking for financing, partners, suppliers, managers, or other objectives specific to your type of business.

C2 PRESENTATION TIPS: Communicating with your finished plan

Use the following tips as a checklist to ensure that the hard work you have done in assembling information for your idea is not wasted due to a mistaken perception of a potential reader or evaluator.

Third Person Refer to your business in the third person "it" or by its name rather than using "we." Using "we" when writing comes across as amateurish. Also, avoid catchy phrases such as "fantastic sales" or "incredible product", which can make you sound inexperienced or immature to readers.

Clear Language Keep in mind that your reader may not be technically versed about your product or industry. Try to use clear, simple language to describe overly technical matters. Friends and acquaintances can provide valuable feedback on the clarity of your plan.

Know Your Audience You may not want each reader to see the same content. For example, if you have given a copy of your plan to a potential manager or customer, you likely do not want the individual to know intimate details of your profit and cash flow projections. This can be made easier by keeping your plan on a computer allowing you to make alterations for certain readers.

> **Use clear, simple language to ensure you are understood.**

Bullet Points Use bullet points to simply and concisely explain certain sections that do not require much explanation or to reinforce key points. Individuals can save time by referring to these points instead of continually long paragraphs.

Legal Concern If you are concerned about revealing the idea to others, put a clause on the first page similar to the following sentence. "*This document is the property of _____ (insert company or owner's name) and contains confidential information which may not be disclosed or reproduced without permission of _____ (same name)*". A lawyer can help you draft a similar clause.

Repeating Yourself Do not be afraid to repeat yourself since the reader may just skim your plan without reading certain sections and miss key points otherwise.

Irrelevant Sections Some things that do not appear to be important to include can be important if they help to explain the idea further for a reader. For example, a section entitled "OPERATIONS PERSONNEL" can be used to state that no personnel is required. This helps the evaluator understand that no employee costs are incurred. If you are unsure as to whether to leave a section in or out, err on the side of caution and keep it in since it will show that you have addressed the issue and not simply forgotten or ignored it.

Length The average plan is approximately 8-20 pages including Table of Contents and Appendices. Some highly technical products with complicated specifications or manufacturing procedures can be 25-50 pages in length. Anything over 30 pages and readers may feel as though they have been forced to read the telephone book.

Presentation Presentation can create an image of professionalism. Once you have completed the steps in this book, the plan can be transferred to blank (8 1/2 by 11) sheets of paper by typewriter or word processor. For details on available software that allows you to answer the questions on your computer, automatically prepares a written plan, and calculates your financial statements, contact the publisher, Envision Communications Ltd., at the address in the front of the guide.

APPENDIX **D**:

Legal Considerations

There are three main forms of business ownership: *sole proprietorship, partnership* and *corporation.* The descriptions, advantages, and disadvantages below are for discussion purposes only. A lawyer or accountant can properly advise as to what form best suits your type of business and tax situation.

D1 FORM OF OWNERSHIP: Sole Proprietorship

Since an individual is obligated by law to register if carrying on a business, many individual entrepreneurs start their business as a s*ole proprietorship.* This is the easiest and most inexpensive form of business to start. There is no legal separation between the company and the individual and, consequently, the income of the business is considered the income of the individual and taxed at the appropriate individual rate. Therefore, the owner would not pay themselves a salary. A key characteristic of this type of ownership is that the owner is held personally responsible for all debts and contracts of the business, meaning that creditors can sue you personally to collect. This is known as *unlimited liability* since the business debt is not limited to the business itself but is also the personal responsibility of the individual.

> **Main Advantages Of A Sole Propietorship**
>
> - Authority to make all decisions
> - Low start-up cost
> - All profits go to the owner
>
> **Main Disadvantage Of A Sole Propietorship**
>
> - Personally liable for debts of the business

D2 FORM OF OWNERSHIP: Partnership

1. General Partnership There are two forms of partnerships. The first, known as a *general partnership*, is when two or more people combine their skills and assets to form and run a business. Each partner is entitled to a share of the profits and losses. The percentage each receives is based on a *Partnership Agreement* which should be formally prepared and signed between the partners. Other issues that can be (but are not necessarily) contained in this agreement are such things as how partners can be added, what happens in the event of death, and the role of each partner in the business. Regardless of the details of this Partnership Agreement, each partner is *fully liable* for repaying all debts of the business, regardless of the initial amount invested in the partnership or whether the business debts were incurred by another partner. Therefore, general partnerships are similar to sole proprietorship as *both* have the characteristic of *unlimited liability*.

> **Main Advantages of General Partnerships**
>
> - Multiple partners creates more resources
> - More owners may mean more expertise
> - Low start-up costs
>
> **Main Disadvantages of General Partnerships**
>
> - Any partner can be held liable for full debt of business (unlimited liability)
> - Divided authority can cause disagreements

2. *Limited Partnership* The second type of partnership is a *limited partnership*. This is a partnership where some partners (referred to as *limited partners*) do not wish to be held personally liable for the debts incurred by the business. However, in return for this guarantee the limited partners have no decision-making authority or participation in the running of the business. Instead, a *general partner* holds all decision-making authority, but is also held personally liable for *all* debts of the business. A limited partnership is often used in instances where investors put money into a business but are not involved in the day-to-day operation. Similar to a general partnership, details of how profits are shared are outlined in a Partnership Agreement.

> **Main Advantage of Limited Partnerships**
>
> • Better ability to attract investors as they would have limited liability
>
> **Main Disadvantage of Limited Partnerships**
>
> • General Partner alone liable for debts of the business

D3 FORM OF OWNERSHIP: Corporation

A *corporation* is considered an *entity* and can, therefore, operate as any individual would in borrowing money, entering into contracts, filing a tax return, and so forth. Corporations have continuous existence even if the owners become deceased. The key distinguishing characteristic is that owners of corporations *cannot* be held personally liable for the debts of the corporation should the corporation not be able to pay. This is known as *limited liability* since the liability is limited to the corporation. However, banks usually require that loans to new corporations be *personally* guaranteed by the owner which effectively nullifies limited liability in respect to the bank loans. Also, profits of a corporation are not considered to be the owners' income. Owners are instead paid a salary and are only taxed on that employment income. If there is a profit after the corporation pays all expenses, including its taxes and owners' salaries, and the owners wish to take more money out of the corporation, the extra money is declared as *dividend income* by the owner who must then pay tax on it. Therefore, the dividends are taxed twice, once as a profit of the corporation and then as dividend income of the owner. Corporations involve more paperwork than other forms of ownership and are more expensive to start.

> **Main Advantages of Corporations**
>
> • Limited liability
> • Continuous existence
> • Possible tax advantages
>
> **Main Disadvantages of Corporations**
>
> • Dividends are taxed twice
> • More expensive to start
> • Increased paperwork

Example

A business was founded as a limited partnership by Lisa, John and Mary. Lisa, the general manager, and John, the marketing manager, will both be general partners. Mary, an investor and limited partner, contributed 25% of the startup money. As a limited partner, she will not be involved in the day-to-day operations. Partnership Agreement details are summarized below.

PARTNERSHIP DETAILS

Name	% Contribution	% Profits	Positon/Occupation
• Mary	• 25 %	• 30 %	• Investor & Limited Partner • Not involved in operations
• Lisa	• 40 %	• 35 %	• General Manager • Manages daily operations
• John	• 35 %	• 35 %	• Marketing Manager

Optional Planning Questions Appendix D

NOTE: The answers can be inserted into the Section 1A Owners.

1. What form of ownership will your business likely have (sole proprietorship, partnership, or incorporation) and why? Will this form of ownership change?

2. Who are the individual owners, what is their role in the business and how will they be reimbursed?

3. Is there a written agreement outlining all of the owners' participation (such as a Partnership Agreement)?

Evaluator's Thoughts

The evaluator is interested in each owner's role in the business and the kind of financial resources the owners have to support the business in its initial stages. Evaluators also consider whether the product or business represent potential liability for the owners that could be avoided by incorporating.

D4 LEGAL PROTECTION: Protecting your idea

There are several legal issues regarding protection of a business and its customers. Here are some issues that may affect you if you are just starting out. Since these special issues revolve around the protection of your idea, you should consult a lawyer to ensure that the proper protection is offered.

Exclusive Rights, Franchising, Licensing are issues typical in retailing, service businesses, or franchise ownership. Someone who has been given the *exclusive right* to sell a brand of product or service in a certain region is legally protected from other individuals offering those same products or services for sale. Before accepting the rights to a franchise agreement or exclusive rights to a product, you should ensure that the grantor of these has guaranteed in writing that there is a defined territory for which you have the rights. It certainly does not help your business prospects if another business in close proximity were offering the same "exclusive" products.

Perhaps you see the potential *licensing* or *franchising* of your idea to others to expand your potential revenues. For those wishing further reading on any of these issues, there are dozens of books in libraries under the subject "franchising" or "licensing" offering tips on evaluating or offering these types of opportunities. If anyone is offering you the rights to a franchise, you should ensure that the company making the offer has a business plan similar in form to the one in this guide. Their plan should describe each of the major business areas (represented by the chapters in this guide) of the franchise opportunity. Good companies looking for franchisees will not turn down your request for extensive information, and will likely include a thorough plan without being asked. This will help you evaluate the company's present operations and future direction, improving your ability to make an informed decision.

Trademarks are denoted by the symbol™ and registered trademarks by a symbol®on the names of products (commonly seen on such things as sports teams logos, brand name products) or well-known phrases (think of any famous phrase associated with a product or company and it is likely the phrase is registered). These are registered to prohibit another business from using the same or similar names and phrases to market their own products. If you have a product that will be known by a certain name, you may want to discuss the availability of the name or phrase with a trademark agent, trademark lawyer, name search firm in the Yellow Pages, or the name registration office.

LEGAL PROTECTION

- Exclusive Rights
- Franchise Agreement
- Licensing Agreement
- Trademarks
- Patents
- Copyrights
- Liability Coverage

Patents are protection for inventors which prohibit others from copying the design of a product and selling it as their own. It usually covers a period of several years. Any invention that could be useful in some application is usually worth patenting since the patent itself can be sold to an existing business even if the person does not plan on ever producing it. Several books on the topic "patents" exist and the lucrative potential of owning a successful patent probably makes further reading worthwhile. Federal patent branch offices, patent lawyers, or patent agents can usually assist you in determining if other similar patents presently exist, what steps are involved in attaining one, and whether it is worthwhile for your product idea to be patented. Check under "patents" or "trademarks" in the telephone book or call the nearest government office specializing in small business.

Copyrights on a book, song, or film can exist automatically upon completion and without registration, but legal registration can provide further legal protection. Most countries have their own procedures, but major international trade agreements guarantee that patents, trademarks, and copyrights are recognized in signatory countries. National libraries have information kits on registering procedures which they will provide to artists and authors.

Liability Another issue worth discussing in this section is the issue of *liability*. Some product manufacturers and service providers have been sued due to performance, misuse, injury, or failure to provide the promised benefits. Although rare, this issue may apply to your idea. It is best to seek the advice of a professional lawyer for issues of product or service liability. Liability risk may necessitate insurance coverage, customer waivers, or some other forms of protection.

APPENDIX E:

Financial Example

The *balance sheet* below was derived from the projected 12-month Lightcost Lighting Income and Cash Flow statements on the following page. Those two statements contain the initials "BS" (for "balance sheet") to the far right of the figures used to construct the balance sheet. The example was originally introduced in Chapter 8A **Income Statement**. Balance sheets are explained on page 86.

ASSETS

Cash $21,000 Simply take the year-end closing cash balance which represents your cash on hand (Line U).

Accounts Receivable $18,500 This asset represents the portion of your sales that remain uncollected. This is derived by taking your Total Sales less the Total Cash Collected from Sales (Line B-Line G). The difference is your cash from sales that you have not yet collected and is known as *Accounts Receivable*.

Truck $13,500 The truck was worth $18,000 when it was bought. After a year it has depreciated (for explanation of depreciation see Section 8A **Income Statement**). Therefore, the value is $18,000 (Line K) less $4500 (Line 10 in Income Statement).

LIGHTCOST LIGHTING PROJECTED BALANCE SHEET, END OF YEAR 1 (all figures in dollars)

ASSETS		
Cash		21000
Accounts Receivable		18500
Original Truck Value 18000		
Less Depreciation 4500		13500
TOTAL ASSETS		53000
LIABILITIES		
Truck Loan		14400
TOTAL LIABILITIES		14400
OWNERS' EQUITY		
Retained Earnings		38600
TOTAL EQUITY		38600
TOTAL LIABILITIES & EQUITY		53000

LIABILITIES

Truck Loan $14,400 Philip's business has a loan outstanding of $18,000 at the beginning of the year (Line H). Looking at his repayment of principal on the loan (Line L), he has repaid $3600 in principal over the year. Therefore, take $18,000 (Line H) less $3600 (Line L) to arrive at the $14,400 year-end loan balance figure. Remember, loan *interest* payments do not reduce the original amount of a loan and so are not relevant in coming up with the loan balance.

> *NOTE: Since suppliers are paid cash upon delivery and the installation company is paid immediately upon completion of a job, there are no outstanding amounts owing to these parties. If these suppliers were paid on credit, outstanding amounts would be considered monies owing and, consequently, would appear as Accounts Payable in the Liabilities section.*

EQUITY

Retained Earning $38,600 Profit at year end is $38,600. This amount when retained in the company becomes equity in the business and is known as shareholders' or owners' equity. It is derived from the Income Statement, Line 13.

TOTAL

As in the balance sheet on this page, Equity ($38,600), when added to Liabilities ($14,400) always equal the Total Assets ($53,000) of any business. This general rule can be remembered by the acronym "ALE" for "Assets + Liabilities = Equity". This is similar to taking the value of a house and subtracting the amount of the mortgage to determine the owner's equity in the house.

Lightcost Lighting Projected Income Statement

Month 1-Month 12 Year 1

							MONTH								
		1	**2**	**3**	**4**	**5**	**6**	**7**	**8**	**9**	**10**	**11**	**12**	**TOTAL**	
1	**Sales**	**2500**	**2500**	**7500**	**10000**	**7500**	**7500**	**10000**	**7500**	**7500**	**7500**	**10000**	**10000**	**90000**	
2	Less cost of installers fees	700	700	2100	2800	2100	2100	2800	2100	2100	2100	2800	2800	25200	
3	Less cost of lights	300	300	900	1200	900	900	1200	900	900	900	1200	1200	10800	
4	**TOTAL Cost of sales**	**1000**	**1000**	**3000**	**4000**	**3000**	**3000**	**4000**	**3000**	**3000**	**3000**	**4000**	**4000**	**36000**	
5	**Gross Profit**	**1500**	**1500**	**4500**	**6000**	**4500**	**4500**	**6000**	**4500**	**4500**	**4500**	**6000**	**6000**	**54000**	BS
	OPERATING EXPENSES														
6	Rent	300	300	300	300	300	300	300	300	300	300	300	300	3600	
7	Insurance	100	100	100	100	100	100	100	100	100	100	100	100	1200	
8	Interest	125	125	125	125	125	125	125	125	125	125	125	125	1500	
9	Advertising	400	400	400	300	400	200	200	200	200	400	400	400	3900	
10	Depreciation	375	375	375	375	375	375	375	375	375	375	375	375	4500	
11	Telephone	75	75	75	75	50	50	50	50	50	50	50	50	700	
12	**TOTAL EXPENSES**	**1375**	**1375**	**1375**	**1275**	**1350**	**1150**	**1150**	**1150**	**1150**	**1350**	**1350**	**1350**	**15400**	
13	**NET PROFIT**	**125**	**125**	**3125**	**4725**	**3150**	**3350**	**4850**	**3350**	**3350**	**3150**	**4650**	**4650**	**38600**	BS

Lightcost Lighting Projected Cash Flow Statement

Month 1-Month 12 Year 1

							MONTH								
		1	**2**	**3**	**4**	**5**	**6**	**7**	**8**	**9**	**10**	**11**	**12**	**TOTAL**	
A	**Opening Cash Balance**	**0**	**-2300**	**-3850**	**-6150**	**-7350**	**-4375**	**300**	**3225**	**7400**	**12075**	**15800**	**18025**		
B	**Estimated Sales**	**2500**	**2500**	**7500**	**10000**	**7500**	**7500**	**10000**	**7500**	**7500**	**7500**	**10000**	**10000**	**90000**	BS
	CASH INFLOWS														
C	Cash Sales (0%)	0	0	0	0	0	0	0	0	0	0	0	0	0	
D	Collection of Acc. Rec. due in 30 days (30%)	0	750	750	2250	3000	2250	2250	3000	2250	2250	2250	3000	24000	
E	Collection of Acc. Rec. due in 60 days (50%)	0	0	1250	1250	3750	5000	3750	3750	5000	3750	3750	3750	35000	
F	Collection of Acc. Rec. due in 90 days (20%)	0	0	0	**500**	500	1500	2000	1500	1500	2000	1500	1500	12500	
G	Total Cash Collected from Sales	0	750	2000	4000	7250	8750	8000	8250	8750	8000	7500	8250	71500	BS
H	Truck Loan Proceeds Received	18000	0	0	0	0	0	0	0	0	0	0	0	18000	BS
I	Total Cash Received	18000	750	2000	4000	7250	8750	8000	8250	8750	8000	7500	8250	89500	
J	**Total Available Cash (A+I)**	**18000**	**-1550**	**-1850**	**-2150**	**-100**	**4375**	**8300**	**11475**	**16150**	**20075**	**23300**	**26275**		
	CASH OUTFLOWS														
K	Purchase of Truck	18000	0	0	0	0	0	0	0	0	0	0	0	18000	BS
L	Truck Loan Principal Loan Payment	300	300	300	300	300	300	300	300	300	300	300	300	3600	BS
M	Truck Loan Interest on Payment	125	125	125	125	125	125	125	125	125	125	125	125	1500	BS
N	Installers Fees ($700 per floor)	700	700	2100	2800	2100	2100	2800	2100	2100	2100	2800	2800	25200	
O	Cost of lights ($300 per floor)	300	300	900	1200	900	900	1200	900	900	900	1200	1200	10800	
P	Rent	300	300	300	300	300	300	300	300	300	300	300	300	3600	
Q	Insurance	100	100	100	100	100	100	100	100	100	100	100	100	1200	
R	Advertising	400	400	400	300	400	200	200	200	200	400	400	400	3900	
S	Telephone	75	75	75	75	50	50	50	50	50	50	50	50	700	
T	**Total Outflows**	**20300**	**2300**	**4300**	**5200**	**4275**	**4075**	**5075**	**4075**	**4075**	**4275**	**5275**	**5275**	**68500**	
U	**Closing Cash Balance (J-T)**	**-2300**	**-3850**	**-6150**	**-7350**	**-4375**	**300**	**3225**	**7400**	**12075**	**15800**	**18025**	**21000**		BS

NOTE: Closing Cash Balance each month becomes the opening cash balance for the next month.

The Idea Guide

INDEX

NOTES